Lessons for parents from a perfect parent

Lessons for parents from a perfect parent

The Meaning of God as Father to His Children

Jim Barclay

© 2006 by Jim Barclay. All rights reserved.
2nd Printing 2014

Trusted Books is an imprint of Deep River Books. The views expressed or implied in this work are those of the author. To learn more about Deep River Books, go online to www.DeepRiverBooks.com.

No part of this publication may be reproduced, stored in a retrieval system or transmitted in any way by any means—electronic, mechanical, photocopy, recording or otherwise—without the prior permission of the copyright holder, except as provided by USA copyright law.

All Scriptures are taken from New American Standard Bible, © 1960, 1963, 1968, 1971, 1972, 1973, 1975, 1977 by The Lockman Foundation. Used by permission.

ISBN: 978-1-63269-011-1
Library of Congress Catalog Card Number: 2006900717

I would like to thank Mr. Marvin Lane, a friend of almost 40 years, for his editing this book and for his words of encouragement.

I would also like to thank Dr. Steve Brown of Key Life Network for his reading and graciously endorsing this book.

Dedication

This book is dedicated to my beloved
twin sons, Andy and Mike,
my glory and joy.
It is also dedicated to my parents,
Jess and Mary Barclay,
who exhibited many of the
principles in this book as
they raised my brother, Reed,
and me.

Table of Contents

Prologue — xi

1. Treating Your Children As Though They Were Adopted — 15
2. Providing an Atmosphere of Security for Your Children — 27
3. Being a Source of Comfort to Your Children — 41
4. Being There for Your Children — 55
5. Teaching Your Children through Discipline — 71
6. Teaching Your Children through Instruction and Example — 93
7. Demonstrating Grace and Compassion to Your Children — 117
8. Being an Encourager to Your Children — 137
9. Loving Your Children Unconditionally — 153
10. Praying for Your Children — 169

Epilogue — 195
Endnotes — 201

Prologue

Several years ago a friend of mine arranged for both of us to have lunch with Steve Brown of Key Life Network. Steve is a very gracious and loving man who made us both feel like we were the most important people in the world at that time. During our lunch we began talking about our families. At that time my twin sons were in their late teens and Steve's children were young adults. We both realized how gracious God had been to us because our children had never really caused us any problems and they were great children and a real blessing. Steve then made a comment that we should write a book about raising children.

Well, I sure don't feel qualified to write a book about parenting based upon my parenting skills. I'm afraid that my sons have turned out good in spite of me, rather than as a result of me. As stated previously, truly God has been gracious in how my sons have turned out. I could think of many parents who would be better role models than I when it comes to parenting. Whenever we want to look to a person as a role model or an example to follow in a particular skill, we probably look for the best at what they do. In other words, we want to imitate the best. For example, if I wanted to learn basketball, I would probably seek to imitate Michael

Jordan. If I wanted to become a good golfer, I would seek to imitate Tiger Woods. Now it is very unlikely that any of us would ever reach the level of a Michael Jordan in basketball or a Tiger Woods in golf. Why would we seek to imitate them, then? The higher the standard that we do aim for, the better we will become. But we need to realize something very important. As good a basketball player as Michael Jordan is and as good a golfer as Tiger Woods is, neither of them is perfect in their particular sport. There is always room for improvement. That is why you hear of them practicing so much. The same is true of parents. Regardless of whom we may seek to imitate as parents, they will be far from perfect. I have some good news, however. There is a perfect parent we can seek to imitate. It is God our heavenly Father. Fortunately, more is now being written concerning God as our Father and we can never exhaust this wonderful truth from Scripture. Consequently, in this book we will focus on the aspect of God as a Perfect Parent to His children. Now I know that the word "parent" is never used of God as our Father in Scripture. The reason I use that word to describe God is that some Scriptures compare God to both an earthly father and mother whereby we can better understand our relationship with Him. In no way do I advocate the movement that uses feminine pronouns or even calls God "our Mother" for that is not biblical. In fact, throughout this book I won't call God a parent but will always refer to Him as our Father in masculine terms. The point is this. Whenever God is described in terms of an earthly father or mother as it relates to their responsibilities, He perfectly portrays them.

The purpose of this book is threefold. First, it is to teach Christians what a great Father that we truly have, for so many don't know this. Oh, they may know it intellectually, but they do not know it in their hearts and through experiencing it in everyday life. Many times the reason they don't know it in their hearts and experience is because of their relationship with their earthly father. Professional counselors have stated that one of the reasons teenage girls become sexually active is because of a lack of emotional support, care and love from their fathers. No. This is not to say that such girls have no responsibility for their sinful actions. They are totally responsible for their choices, but an improper relationship with their father is often a contributing factor to their sin. Such is not confined to girls, though. One of my instructors in seminary stated that growing up, he had a bad relationship with his father. One day he offered to meet with a group of students over a brown bag lunch. He shared with them of his relationship with his father and he was astonished to learn that well over half of the students present did not have a good relationship with their fathers, either. And this can often lead to an improper understanding and relationship with their heavenly Father. Martyn Lloyd Jones wrote, "If you should ask me to state in one phrase what I regard as the greatest defect in most Christians' lives I would say that it is our failure to know God as our Father as we should know Him. If only we got hold of this, we could smile in the face of every possibility and eventuality that lies ahead of us."[1]

The second purpose is that hopefully some non-Christians will have their hearts and eyes opened to what a great Father God is through faith in Jesus Christ as their personal Lord and Savior. Just as with Christians, I've also heard of non-Christians who don't want to have anything to do with God as Father based on their experiences with their earthly fathers who may have been mean, abusive, cruel or unloving. This has led some Christians, when talking or counseling with such non-Christians, to hesitate in referring to God as Father and thus, consider referring to Him as Mother. As written previously, I don't think we should refer to God as Mother. Rather, we should tell others that He is a Father like no other and can be totally trusted. He will never abuse His children.

The final purpose is to help parents become better parents to their children by following the principles from the Bible as they relate to God as our Father. These principles are not to be seen as a list of things which seem impossible to do, but to focus on that which flows from a love relationship. Many of these principles overlap and thus, there may seem to be repetition. Also, there will be some Scriptures that are repeated in more than one chapter because Scriptures can have multiple applications. These repetitions are not bad, however, for as I've heard Dr. Stephen Olford state, "It is better to teach one truth seven times than seven truths one time." Now, we will never be able to perfectly imitate our heavenly Father in parental responsibility, but, as written previously, the higher the standard we reach for, the better parents we will become. As my New Testament professor at Reformed Theological Seminary, Dr. Allen Mawhinney wrote of Matthew 5:48, "Therefore you are to be perfect, as your heavenly Father is perfect," there are two possible interpretations of that verse. "Be perfect according to the model of your heavenly Father" or "God's children are to be perfect not only according to the pattern of the Father but because the Father is perfect."[2] Of course, that passage is in the context of loving your enemies, but it would also apply to any aspect of seeking to model or imitate our heavenly Father. May we be found faithful.

Chapter One

Treating Your Children As Though They Were Adopted

> For you have not received a spirit of slavery
> leading to fear again, but you have received
> a spirit of adoption as sons by which
> we cry out, "Abba! Father!"
> —Romans 8:15

I once heard a story about two little boys arguing about something. Of course, with little boys, in most cases, they don't like to lose, regardless of the situation or competition, even an argument. Consequently, they often will do or say something that they feel will put the other one in his place. Such was the case between these two little boys. One of them finally said to the other, "You're adopted and I'm not." The other boy responded, "That's true, but my parents chose me while your parents were stuck with you."

Adoption is a wonderful blessing to many married couples today. Couples that have not had children by natural means have been blessed to adopt children and bring them into their family. That is one of the reasons why it is so sad that there are so many abortions in our society. Those precious aborted babies could have been placed into a family that would want them. Then there are couples who may have had children of their own but also want to adopt more. We often hear of families adopting foreign children and bringing them to America to live with them. Then there are some families who may adopt handicapped children to provide a good home for them. Regardless of the circumstances, adoption is such a blessing to the family and to the adopted child.

As great as adoption is in our society and as much a blessing it is to the family and the child, it does not compare to our being adopted by God. Now, I don't intend for this chapter to be an exhaustive study on the biblical truth of adoption. I would, however, recommend that each Christian study this great truth further and thus, I highly recommend Dr. Robert A. Peterson's outstanding book, *Adopted by God,* published by P&R Publishing Company. I will be sharing some information and stories, however, from Dr. Peterson's book to illustrate the lesson for this chapter. If Christian parents want to learn from our Father, then we must understand and have a grasp of this great truth of biblical adoption and what it means for us, and our children.

The first thing we must consider in reference to adoption is its definition. Different theologians have spoken of adoption in terms of justification, regeneration, and glorification.[1] For the purpose of this chapter we will look at it as it relates to our justification or the beginning of our salvation. Question 34 of the Shorter Catechism of the Westminster Confession asks, "What is adoption?" The answer is, "Adoption is an act of God's free grace, whereby we are received into the number, and have a right to all the privileges of the sons of God." In other words, our adoption means that we are chosen by God to become a member of His family as His sons and daughters. In order to understand the significance of our adoption we must understand our status prior to our adoption.

There is a false teaching that speaks of the universal Fatherhood of God and brotherhood of man. Yes, God is everyone's Father in the sense of His being our Creator. As Paul preached to the men of Athens, as recorded in Acts 17, verse 28, "for in Him we live and move and exist, as even some of your own poets have said, 'for we also are His offspring.'" Spiritually, however, all mankind does not have God as Father in the sense of intimacy and love that is to characterize a family relationship. John 8 records Jesus speaking to Jews who were described as believing in Him. Had they truly believed in Him? He told them that if they were truly His disciples they would abide in His word and thus, know the truth, which would make them free. The Jews were upset with His words and claimed to be Abraham's offspring and thus had never been enslaved to anyone. Jesus told them they were slaves to sin and they did the things which they had heard from their father. Their reply was that Abraham was their father to which Jesus responded, "If you are Abraham's children, do the deeds of Abraham"(v.39). Of course they weren't doing the deeds of Abraham because they were seeking to kill Jesus. Then Jesus plainly tells them in verse 44, "You are of your father, the devil, and you want to do the desires of your father."

That describes the spiritual condition of mankind. As Paul wrote in Ephesians 2:1, man is dead in his trespasses and sins. Consequently, he walks according to the course of this world, according to the prince of the power of the air, and the spirit that is now working in the sons of disobedience (Eph 2:2). As Paul also wrote in 2 Timothy 2:26, man is held captive by Satan to do his will. Therefore, as our theme verse for this chapter states, man is subjected to a spirit of slavery or bondage, which leads to or results in fear. Do you see what this means then? This speaks of the total depravity of man. Because man is depraved and under sin, Paul wrote in Romans 3 that no one is righteous or seeks for God or does good. In other words, there is nothing about us that would make us acceptable to God. In fact, as Romans 5 describes us, we were helpless, ungodly, sinners and even enemies of God. There is nothing in us that God would see as worthy of a relationship with Him. You see then, our situation was extremely desperate and hopeless.

Yet, being in that miserable condition, Paul wrote in Ephesians 1 that God chose us, His children, in Christ before the foundation of the world. In love He predestined us to adoption as sons through

Jesus Christ to Himself. It is important that we understand what this means. It does not mean that God looked down through history and saw that we would choose Him by believing in His Son, the Lord Jesus Christ, but that He, in eternity past, chose us and predestined us to adoption as sons and daughters through Jesus Christ to Himself.

A beautiful picture which depicts this is God's choosing of Israel in the Old Testament. Now, why did God choose Israel? Was it because Israel was so powerful or so good a nation? Not at all. Why then? Deuteronomy 7:7-8 gives the answer. "The LORD did not set His love on you nor choose you because you were more in number than any of the peoples, for you were the fewest of all peoples, but because the LORD loved you and kept the oath which He swore to your forefathers, the LORD brought you out by a mighty hand, and redeemed you from the house of slavery, from the hand of Pharaoh king of Egypt." Did you notice why God chose Israel? Because of His love and thus, in His love He redeemed Israel. Israel, living in bondage and fear, controlled by Pharaoh, was redeemed by God. As God said to Israel as recorded in Isaiah 43:1, "Do not fear, for I have redeemed you; I have called you by name; you are Mine."

So, just as God redeemed Israel from Egyptian bondage, He has redeemed His children whereby we receive the spirit of adoption as sons and thus, can cry out, "Abba! Father!" Well, what do we mean by the word redeem? It means to demand or buy back. It speaks of deliverance. What did we need deliverance from? The bondage and power of Satan and sin. As God said in Isaiah 44:22, "I have wiped out your transgressions like a thick cloud, And your sins like a heavy mist. Return to me, for I have redeemed you." Did you notice that it was God who redeemed us? Why? Because man cannot redeem himself. As Psalm 49:7-8 tells us, "No man can by any means redeem his brother, Or give to God a ransom for him—For the redemption of his soul is costly, And he should cease trying forever."

Now, I want to relate Israel's redemption from Egyptian bondage and our redemption from Satan's bondage of sin to a very important truth. Whenever someone does something for us which may have involved quite an effort to include cost or time, we may say, "You went to a lot of trouble to do this for me." Well, if I may use that phrase, God went to a lot of trouble to redeem Israel and He went to a lot of trouble to redeem you and me whereby we could be adopted into His family. Let's think about that for a moment. What did God do to redeem Israel? There is no way to mention all that He did, but just think of the ten plagues. Each of those plagues demonstrated His power over an Egyptian god. And in the last plague, the death of the first born, He told Israel how they could be spared by sacrificing the Passover Lamb and placing its blood upon the lintels and door posts. Of course, that points to the perfect fulfillment of the Lord Jesus Christ on the cross of Calvary whereby we could be redeemed from Satan's bondage.

As we saw in Isaiah 44:22, it is only God who can redeem us and there was only one price that could be paid. Peter wrote in 1 Peter 1:18-19, "knowing that you were not redeemed with perishable things like silver or gold from your futile way of life inherited from your forefathers, but with precious blood, as of a lamb unblemished and spotless, the blood of Christ." And do you realize, God was pleased to do so. As Isaiah 53:10a tells us, "But the LORD was pleased to crush Him, putting Him to grief." You see then, God went to a lot of trouble to redeem us whereby we could be adopted as His children. Think of all the efforts that Satan went to in the Old Testament to try and prevent God from carrying out His plan of sending the Messiah. And then once Jesus came, we see even more so, Satan trying to destroy God's plan. Yet, God carried it out with perfect faithfulness.

Now, let's carry this thought even further on an individual basis. Think of all the trouble or effort that God went through to redeem you. Think of all the circumstances that He arranged to draw you to Himself. Think of the Christian parents, teachers or friends that had an influence on you. Think of all the prayers that were lifted up for your salvation. Think of all the difficult circumstances that He may have used to get your attention. God went to all this effort and orchestrated it all in order to draw you to Himself through Christ whereby you could be forgiven and adopted into His family as His child. And why did He do this? It wasn't because you or I were special but because He chose to love us. You see, it was not as if God needed more children. He had a Son, a perfect Son, with whom He shared a perfect relationship and fellowship. We needed a Father, but He didn't need children. Yet, He took those who were helpless, ungodly, sinners and His enemies and still adopted us as His children. Why? Here again, He chose to love us even though there was nothing lovely about us. As John wrote in 1 John 3:1, "See how great a love the Father has bestowed upon us, that we should be called children of God; and such we are." Tim Keller wrote, "God now loves us as if we had done all Jesus had done. He loves us even as He loves His own Son...adoption is fundamentally not a change in nature, but a change in status. As in civil adoption, we not only become a loved member of a family, but certain rights and duties come to us legally. Adoption brings us into the most intimate position possible with the God of the universe."[2] Thus, we belong to God and can call Him, "Abba, Father."

As His child, do you know what God your Father thinks of you? He tells us in Isaiah 43:4ab, "Since you are precious in My sight, Since you are honored and I love you." Did you notice what that verse says? First, we are precious in His sight. The word "precious" means prized and is also translated costly, esteemed and valued. Here again, our being precious to our Father is shown by the price He paid to redeem us and adopt us into His family. Second, we are honored. This word means to get honor and glory. It speaks of treating, regarding or practically declaring one as worthy of honor. Finally, He says, "I love you." Notice, there are no strings attached or no conditions. Just, "I love you." Unconditional love. Now, we will examine our Father's love for us in chapter 9, but it is important that we realize now that this love is not a result of merit or worth of the person loved. Rather, it is a love that delights in giving. It is a love that keeps on loving even when the loved one is unresponsive, unkind, unlovable and unworthy. It is a love that has a consuming passion for the well-being of others.

What a great truth and blessing then to be adopted by God our Father. I once saw a sign outside a sports bar that read, "Beer is proof that the Good Lord loves us." That sign broke my heart each time I passed by it. Yet, that is the attitude of the world. As stated previously, the world believes that God is everybody's Father and He will give us what we want to make us happy. Proof that the heavenly Father loves His true children is not beer, but the cross of Calvary whereby we could be adopted into the family of God as we are forgiven of our sin and given the righteousness of Christ. And it is only those who can truly refer to Him as their loving Father.

Now, let's relate this principle to us as parents. You noticed that I entitled this chapter (principle) as "Treating Your Children as Though They Were Adopted." Why would this principle be stated in this way? In order to better understand this, I want to share two testimonies from Peterson's book mentioned before. The first one is from Patrick. He stated, "I happen actually to have been adopted as an infant, so the doctrine of adoption is especially real to me. Briefly, it means that while I was without a future, a hope, even a family to belong to, somebody gave me all of these and more. And this was done, not because of anything I could ever give back in return for such a gift, but just because my parents wanted...to express their love to someone. Likewise, according to the Word of God, God the Father chose me and adopted me, so He could love me. I will never fully understand why my parents or God chose me. But I am forever humbled and just plain amazed that they did."[3]

Then there is the testimony of Chrishon who was born addicted to crack because of his mother's drug habit. He stated, "Coming from an extended family that has adopted many children, the biblical concept of adoption is very warming for me. My relatives who adopted kids did so simply because they desired to. And they did so of their own free choosing; they were not obligated to do so... What is so awesome is that, according to Scripture, before I was even born, God had chosen to adopt me. That is so comforting to me because it means no matter how bad I mess up, God loves me despite myself. And that's what adoption really is—genuine love. I know because I see it in my relatives. In human terms, it is only genuine love that can lead parents to adopt babies born addicted to crack. Human reason can't explain that...My relatives could have chosen a "perfect" child to adopt and been all right. But they chose perhaps the hardest kids to adopt. They had to fight agencies that didn't like white families adopting black kids (not to mention the social persecution they faced) and doctors who told them to put the babies in institutions because they couldn't be controlled and would never be productive. But my relatives displayed true love, sacrificing sleep, money, time, etc., all to love their adopted child.

'God did even more. We all are like crack babies: born helpless, in circumstances beyond our control. There is nothing redeeming about us. But God's genuine love led Him to sacrifice His Son, so that we might be made His sons and daughters.'"[4]

Did you notice what both of those testimonies had in common? Choosing and loving. And did you notice in Chrishon's testimony that he spoke of the difficulties (i.e. all the trouble) that his parents went through in order to adopt him? That is true for any adoption. There is the time element, the financial expense, the lawyers, the agencies and all the paper work. But for the adoptive parents, it is no trouble because of their love for the child.

That is the point of this principle. All parents should treat their children as though they were adopted. In other words, treat them and love them as if you had personally chosen them to be your children. Now, I'm sure that most parents would say they do that, but sadly some of our statements and our actions to our children and others can depict otherwise. Please realize, I'm not talking about those parents who are abusive to their children whether it be verbally or physically. Their actions speak loud and clear that they really don't want or love their children. Rather, I'm talking about those of us who would be seen by others as good parents, but yet we overlook certain areas that can hurt our children. I want to give you several examples of what I mean.

Treating Your Children As Though They Were Adopted

The first example depicts those who have had the number of children that they thought they wanted and then, later in life, they unexpectedly get pregnant again. Do you know how that unexpected child is often referred to later in life? "This is our mistake child." What does that say to the child? If left up to us, we would not have chosen to have you. And invariably, these children often act as if they knew they weren't wanted by their parents and thus, get into all kinds of mischief and trouble.

A second example is the parents that may have had two, three or even more children and they all happen to be the same sex. So, they decide to have one more child trying to get a child of the opposite sex, but the child is also the same sex as the previous children. Unfortunately, the parents' disappointment can speak volumes to that last child. And often the parents may say, "This was suppose to be our boy or girl." Consequently, that child may feel unwanted and could never please their parents because they weren't the right sex.

A third example is the parents that have had several children and the last one may have presented more challenges in raising than the previous children. Many times you will hear a parent say, "If I would have had this child first, I may not have had any more children," or in a joking way say to others, "will you please take this child for me and raise him or her?" I'm afraid, however, that the child will not take such statements as a joke. The child may take it that if my parents had the choice, they would not want me.

A final example is the parents who have one child that may be more talented or gifted than the other children or behaves better than the others and thus, is always depicted as the child who can do no wrong before the other brothers and sisters. You often hear statements as, "Why can't you be more like your brother or sister?" In other words, the parents depict partiality toward this child and it causes undue pressure on the other children because they don't feel like they can measure up. As a young boy I use to enjoy watching the Smothers brothers. They sang and did comedy together. One of their most famous comedy routines was Tom comparing how he was treated by their mother, versus how his brother Dick was treated. It seemed as if the mother only did for Dick and not for Tom. Their dialogue was extremely funny as a comedy routine, but when it occurs in real life, it is not a laughing matter. We have a prime example of this in the Bible between Jacob and Joseph. Genesis 37:3 states that Israel (Jacob) loved Joseph more than all his other sons and as a result Israel made him a varicolored tunic. How did this affect Joseph's brothers? Genesis 37:4 says that they hated Joseph and could not speak to him on friendly terms. Thus, they plotted to kill him, but eventually sold him into slavery because of their envy. Did they not feel as special to Israel as Joseph obviously did?

Thus, the first principle that we can learn from our perfect Father is that we are to treat our children as though they were adopted in that we would have personally chosen them and loved them if it had been left up to us. One other thing to consider regarding this. Do you realize that our Father has chosen for you your children? Here again, think of all the trouble (effort) He went to in order to give you your child(ren). No child is a surprise or mistake to Him. In fact, since Adam and Eve, He has orchestrated all the DNA, the uniting of a particular sperm and egg, throughout the hundreds or thousands of generations to give you each unique child that you have. And as Psalm 127:3 tells us, those children are a gift from Him. It use to always upset me when Ann, my wife, and I would take our twin sons, Andy and Mike, out in public and push them in a stroller as to the reaction of many people with their words. Invariably, when someone saw they were twins, they would say, "Double trouble." Our immediate response was, "No. They're a double blessing." And that blessing was depicted in a song composed by my mother for them. Right after they were born it took awhile for them to get on a regular nightly sleeping schedule. Consequently, for Ann, sleep was very sporadic. Not long after we brought the boys home, Ann had gone a few days without a real good night's sleep. So, my parents came over to spend the night and help out. They ended up being awake all night holding the boys. It was during the night that my mother composed the song for them. The words were as follows:

> "You're a little miracle, from heaven above.
> Just a little miracle, sent from God with love.
> You're a precious little boy, oh how I love you.
> And I love your little brother too."

They heard that song so much that eventually after they learned to talk, they would sing it themselves. Truly, Andy and Mike are a miracle and a gift from a loving Father. And that should be the attitude of every parent for their child(ren). Don't treat them as we saw in the story at the beginning of this chapter as if you were stuck with them. Aren't you thankful that our heavenly Father doesn't treat us, His children, as if He were stuck with us? Aren't you thankful that He doesn't consider us being a part of His family a mistake? Aren't you glad that He doesn't see us as trouble? Remember, there was nothing worthy or good about us that would cause Him to choose us and adopt us into His family. Yet, He did because of His love for us. Parents, let's learn this valuable lesson from our perfect Father and thus, imitate Him.

Chapter Two

Providing an Atmosphere of Security for Your Children

> Then I said to you, "Do not be shocked, nor fear them. The LORD your God who goes before you will Himself fight on your behalf, just as He did for you in Egypt before your eyes, and in the wilderness where you saw how the LORD your God carried you, just as a man carries his son, in all the way which you have walked, until you came to this place." But for all this, you did not trust the LORD your God, who goes before you on your way, to seek out a place for you to encamp, in fire by night and cloud by day, to show you the way in which you should go.
> —Deuteronomy 1:29-33

The book of Deuteronomy is the fifth book of the Pentateuch. It is a reminder to Israel of how God had acted on their behalf and a look forward to what He expected of them in the Promised Land. The five verses that concern us focus on Israel's rebellion at Kadesh-barnea. God had brought them to the edge of the Promised Land and He wanted them to take possession of it. As they were to take possession of the land, they were not to fear or be dismayed (Deut. 1:21). The people requested of Moses that they send men on ahead to spy out the land and bring back word as to which way they should go up and what cities they should enter (Deut. 1:22). So, Moses sent one man from each tribe and they returned saying that the land was a good land, which did flow with milk and honey as God had promised. Yet, ten of the spies came back saying that the people in the land were bigger and taller than they and the cities were fortified. So, they expressed fears and doubts as to entering at that time. In other words, they doubted God's word. Only two of the spies, Joshua and Caleb, stated that they could conquer the land because God had promised it to them. In fact, as we read in verses 29-30 of Deuteronomy 1, Moses told the people they shouldn't fear because just as God had fought for them in Egypt, He would go before them and fight on their behalf. Well, what was the basis for Moses making such a statement? He reminded the people of how they had seen the LORD God carry them and Moses compares that to a man, a father, carrying his son.

So, we want to focus on God carrying Israel and see what we can learn from that as parents. We saw in the previous chapter of God redeeming Israel and now we are concerned with His carrying Israel in the wilderness. A passage that we didn't consider in the previous chapter but is important to consider now is found in Hosea 11. In verses 1,3-4, God says, "When Israel was a youth I loved him, And out of Egypt I called My son...Yet it is I who taught Ephraim to walk, I took them in My arms: But they did not know that I healed them. I led them with cords of a man, with bonds of love, And I became to them as one who lifts the yoke from their jaws; And I bent down and fed them." What is unique about human beings as it relates to their young as opposed to the animal kingdom? The young of humans need constant care and provision for many years while in the animal kingdom, the newborn can walk quickly and take care of themselves in a much shorter time frame. Well, from both Deuteronomy 1 and Hosea 11 we have the focus of God bringing Israel out of Egypt and carrying them in the wilderness. Now, what is the first thing you think of when you hear the word "wilderness"? It is probably difficult circumstances. The term "wilderness" does not cause us to envision a life of luxury and ease. Israel, thus, faced neither luxury nor ease in their wilderness journey but they had God carrying them as a father carries his son. And as God did this, He was preparing Israel to live as His redeemed people. Let's try to understand how God carried Israel.

First of all, God led them. In Deuteronomy 1:33, we saw that God went before them in their journey to seek out a place for them to camp. He led them in a pillar of fire by night and a pillar of cloud by day and thus, showed them the way they should go. It is interesting to realize the direction that God led Israel as they left Egypt. Exodus 13 tells us that God did not lead them by the way of the Philistines even though it was near. Why did God not want to lead them in that direction? He knew that the people might change their minds when they saw war and long to return to Egypt. Thus, He led them by the way of the wilderness. This demonstrates His wisdom as He led them.

Not only did He lead them by His wisdom, but He also protected them as He led them. Shortly after Israel's departure from Egypt, God hardened Pharaoh's heart to pursue Israel and try to recapture them. When Pharaoh drew near, the Israelites became frightened. To put it in modern terms, Israel was between a rock and a hard place. They had the Red Sea on one side and Pharaoh's army on the other side. It appeared as if they had no way of escape. So, they did the only thing they knew how to do and were good at. They complained to Moses as to why he led them into the wilderness to die. It would have been better to serve the Egyptians in bondage than to die following the LORD in the wilderness. Moses, however, told them not to fear, but to stand by and see the salvation of the LORD which He will accomplish as He fights on their behalf. And we remember well what God did. He parted the Red Sea and Israel went across on dry ground and when Egypt tried to pursue, God caused their chariot wheels to swerve and drive with difficulty. Then He brought back the waters upon Egypt and destroyed them. There are many examples of God protecting Israel, which demonstrated His care and concern for them. As Isaiah wrote, in all of Israel's affliction, God was afflicted too(Isa. 63:9). And in Zechariah, God says of Israel, "for he who touches you, touches the apple of His eye" (Zech. 2:8). So, God carried Israel as He led them and protected them.

Secondly, God carried Israel by providing for their physical needs. In Exodus 15, Israel came to Marah and could not drink the waters because they were bitter. Moses cried out to the LORD and the LORD showed Moses a tree that when he threw it into the waters, they became sweet. Exodus 16 records God providing manna and meat for them. Then Exodus 17 records that when Israel camped at Rephidim there was no water at all for the people to drink. Here again, the people grumbled and complained as to why had Moses brought them out from Egypt to kill them, their children and livestock with thirst. When Moses cried out to God, God had Moses strike the rock at Horeb and water came out of it for the people to drink.

Have you ever thought about what it took to provide for Israel in the wilderness? I received an e-mail from a friend in which the Quartermaster General in the Army calculated what was required to meet Israel's needs in the wilderness. Each day they would need 1500 tons of food which was the equivalent of two freight trains each a mile long. What about water? If they only used enough water to drink and wash a few dishes, that would require 11 million gallons each day. To supply that much water would require a freight train with tank cars 1800 miles long. I mentioned previously God's protection of Israel as they crossed the Red Sea. Let's assume that God had only parted the Red Sea wide enough that they crossed double file. If such was the case, the line would have been 800 miles long and would require 35 days and nights to get through. To cross in the time that Israel actually crossed in would mean that the Red Sea was parted three miles wide whereby they could walk 5000 abreast. I also mentioned previously from Deuteronomy 1:33 that God went before Israel to seek out a place for them to camp.

To accommodate that many people would require a campground two-thirds the size of the state of Rhode Island. You see then, God carried His son, Israel, by providing for his needs.

A third way in which God carried Israel was through the laws and ordinances that He gave them. Nehemiah 9 records Israel being assembled with fasting, sackcloth, and dirt upon them. They had separated themselves from all foreigners and confessed their sins and the iniquities of their fathers. They spent one-fourth of the day reading from the book of the law of the LORD their God and one-fourth of the day confessing and worshiping Him. Then they blessed the LORD God by recalling His great acts on their behalf. And one of His great acts on their behalf was to come down to them on Mount Sinai and give them just ordinances, true laws, and good statutes, and commandments. Why was this such a blessing to Israel? Because of the effect it could have upon them. As David wrote of God's laws, testimony, precepts, commandment, and judgments in Psalm 19, their effect includes: restoring the soul, making wise the simple, rejoicing the heart, enlightening the eyes and providing a true and righteous standard for the people to follow. By following God's law they would demonstrate that they were truly God's own possession.

A final way in which God carried Israel was in the patience He exhibited toward them. We've seen previously of Israel complaining while in the wilderness. If you examine the Scriptures, there were numerous other occasions in which Israel complained about their situation in the wilderness. In fact, it was one complaint after another. It was as if they were never pleased and when God did do something that pleased them, the time of not complaining was short-lived until they faced another difficult situation. The Puritans felt that one of the greatest sins that the people of God can commit is complaining because they are complaining against the circumstances that their sovereign God has ordained for them to experience. Yet, Israel continued to complain and still God was patient with them. Then we remember their sin of making the golden calf. God told Moses that His anger was going to burn against them and destroy them and make of Moses a great nation. Moses, though, interceded and God relented of doing harm to them. In fact, in Exodus 33, God tells Moses that He would send an angel before them to the Promised Land and drive out their enemies, but He would not go up in their midst for Israel was an obstinate people. Here again, Moses interceded by saying that if God's presence did not go with them, then he did not want God to lead them any further. God told Moses that because he had found favor in His sight and had known Moses by name, His presence would go with them. So, truly God was patient with Israel.

We must also realize, however, that there was a limit to God's patience. Remember the time frame of Deuteronomy. Israel was in the fortieth year of their wilderness journey. Now, why had they been in the wilderness so long? Let's focus again on the emphasis of the context of Deuteronomy 1:29-33. It was the sending out of the twelve spies. Ten spies came back and said they should not go up to the land, regardless of God's promise, because the people were much bigger and the cities were fortified. Only Joshua and Caleb said go forward because of God's promise. Even with all the complaining and disobedience, God had patiently dealt with Israel and brought them to the edge of the Promised Land. Yet, with this refusal to trust Him, God's patience ran out. That generation, from twenty years and older, except for Joshua and Caleb, would die in the wilderness and never enter the land that flowed with milk and honey. Those, however, who were under twenty, God would carry into the land.

So, in all these ways we have seen how God truly carried Israel, His son, that He had redeemed from Egyptian bondage. Now, when you combine all these great examples together, what do they point to? God provided an atmosphere of security for Israel even in the wilderness. Sadly, for the most part, Israel did not trust God, but as He carried them, He was providing them the security they needed as they faced difficult circumstances.

This great truth is also depicted in Jesus' teaching as recorded in Matthew's gospel. Dr. Allen Mawhinney wrote, "The thought that

God is a knowing, caring, revealing, forgiving and giving Father provided the basis for Jesus' responses to some of the most basic questions in life."[1] Two particular passages I want to emphasize. In Matthew 6:25-34, Jesus focuses on our not being anxious about the most essential needs of this life, nourishment and protection. Verse 26 tells us that our heavenly Father feeds the birds of the air and we are much more important than they. Then in verse 31 Jesus speaks of not being anxious over what to eat, drink or clothe ourselves with. And just as in verse 26, in verse 32, Jesus emphasizes that our heavenly Father knows that we need all these things. Did you notice the emphasis of the Father in those verses? Jesus did not speak of God as the Father of the birds, but of His children. Dr. Mawhinney wrote, "'Father' is here a name of redemption, not of creation. Jesus tells God's children, 'Your Father feeds them.' The implication is that 'your Father will much more feed you.'"[2] So, our Father will supply our basic needs.

A second passage in Matthew's gospel emphasizes that our Father provides security for us when we are persecuted. In Matthew 10:28-31, Jesus tells us that we are not to fear those who only can kill the body but cannot kill the soul. Rather, we are to fear Him who can destroy both body and soul in hell. In order to encourage His followers then, in verses 29-31 Jesus says, "Are not two sparrows sold for a cent? And yet not one of them will fall to the ground apart from your Father. But the very hairs of your head are all numbered. Therefore do not fear; you are of more value than many sparrows." Here again, Jesus does not call God the Father of the sparrows, but "your Father." Dr. Mawhinney is again very helpful when he writes, "No bird ever dies except by your Father's will...It doesn't say no bird ever dies without your Father knowing it, as though His knowledge were reflexive, a result of death. No, it says no bird dies [literally] 'without your Father' (v.29). Most translators supply 'the will of' or 'the involvement of.' Do you feel the force of it? Not only does your Father have full knowledge, but He is fully involved in your life...Do not fear."[3] What an atmosphere of security that ought to be for the child of God.

Just as God our Father provides for us, His children redeemed from the bondage of sin, an atmosphere of security, parents are to do the same for their children. We looked at four examples of that related to God carrying Israel in the wilderness. Now we want to look at those same four areas as they relate to parents carrying their children today. First, we are to lead and protect them. How do we best do that? By showing them that we are totally dependent upon our Father for His wisdom to make it through life. What this really speaks of is demonstrating to your children that you fear(reverence) your Father and that you seek to trust Him in every aspect of life. This is depicted in two passages in Proverbs. Proverbs 9:10a states, "The fear of the LORD is the beginning of wisdom." And a passage that many of us have learned from childhood, Proverbs 3:5-7, says, "Trust in the LORD with all your heart, And do not lean on your own understanding. In all your ways acknowledge Him, And He will make your paths straight. Do not be wise in your own eyes: Fear the LORD and turn away from evil." Now, what do we mean by wisdom? Whereas we associate knowledge with the knowing of facts or truth, wisdom is being able to apply those facts or truth to your life. And of course, the only ultimate and authoritative truth is God's word. So, our children need to see us looking to God's word for principles related to the challenges and decisions that we face and then praying for God's guidance as we seek to apply those principles to our everyday lives. As we do this, we are demonstrating to them that we cannot make it in this life on our own. In other words, we are trying to influence our children to also trust the heavenly Father whereby they will be totally dependent upon Him and reverence Him. There is no greater way for us to lead and protect our children.

Several years ago I was talking with a man who claimed to be a Christian. Yet, he said something to me that was extremely shocking. He basically stated that he was not going to try to influence his children in any religious beliefs. He was going to let them grow up and decide for themselves what religion they would follow if any. And truly, he never brought his children to worship services with him even though one of them was younger and would not go anywhere unless taken by her dad. Upon reflecting on his statement, I was reminded of Paul's words in Ephesians 4. He wrote of building up the body of Christ "until we all attain to the unity of the faith, and of the knowledge of the Son of God, to a mature man, to the measure of the stature which belongs to the fulness of Christ" (v.13). Why did Paul want the body of Christ to grow to spiritual maturity? So that they would not be children, "tossed here and there by waves, and carried about by every wind of doctrine, by the trickery of men, by craftiness in deceitful scheming"(v.14). What characterizes children based upon Paul's words? They are easily influenced. Just think of the Christmas season with all the commercials on television. A child will see one commercial and just have to have what was depicted in that commercial until the next commercial comes on and grabs his attention. And with all the worldly and ungodly influences that our children are confronted with, they need direction. I would think that most parents who claim to be Christians would agree to the importance that God should play in a person's life, even though they may not always display that themselves. Yet, to say that they are going to let their child(ren) grow up and decide for themselves what they will believe without trying to influence them, I feel, is a form of child abuse. Earlier in the chapter we saw that the young of human beings need constant care and provision for many years. To not lead our children by trying to influence them for God really shows no care and concern for the gift that God has given us. We also saw previously of God carrying Israel in the wilderness and we mentioned that when we think of a wilderness, we think of difficult circumstances. I don't have to tell anyone how difficult life can be. We all have experienced its difficulties to various degrees. Do you want to help your child(ren) to get through these difficult circumstances as best as possible? Lead them by demonstrating that you are totally dependent upon your heavenly Father for His wisdom for the challenges and opportunities of this life.

A few years ago I heard about a friend whose son was playing T-ball. This is baseball for the youngest children. The ball is placed on a waist high tee for the batter to hit rather than being pitched to. One of the most important positions on the field for T-ball is where the pitcher stands because so many balls are hit there. My friend's son played the pitcher's position and thus, many balls were hit to him and he had to decide what play to make. Of course, he was hearing teammates, coaches and parents all hollering where to throw the ball. Unfortunately, he got confused and made several mistakes. After the game the father was trying to encourage his son. The son then made a statement to his father. He stated that he could distinguish his father's voice from every other voice. So, at the next game, when the ball was hit to him, he would listen for his father's direction and do what the father said. What was that young boy saying? "Dad, I trust you and I feel secure in doing what you tell me to do." We can provide that same security in the lives of our children by demonstrating to them that we are totally dependent upon the heavenly Father for His wisdom through His word and prayer in order to make it through the wildernesses that we must face.

Then we saw that this leading also includes protection. Of course, by demonstrating reverence and trust in our Father we are protecting our children, but I want to focus on another aspect of protecting them. It involves being willing to be seen as "the bad guy." Let me explain. Let's see this from two different aspects. First, many times our children are confronted with situations that they don't really want to be in but don't know how to get out of. I'm sure that peer pressure has always been a challenge, but such is especially true in our society today, even in Christian circles and even among younger children. Just because an activity is sponsored by Christians or a church, does not mean that it is wise for our children to attend. Many so-called Christian activities are very worldly and can have a negative influence on our children. Yes, parents want their children to mature to the point that they can stand up against peer pressure and say "no" to certain things, but such does not occur overnight. Consequently, the parent needs to be willing to say "no" for his children and be seen as "the bad guy" in his children's friends' eyes as a means of protection. Let me illustrate. Let's assume that your child is invited to an activity that your child may not feel comfortable going to, but is being pressured by friends to attend. The parent can take the pressure off the child by being the one who says that the child cannot attend.

A second aspect of this is that the parent must also be willing to be seen as "the bad guy" in his own child's eyes. Sometimes the child may want to do something that you, as the parent, know they shouldn't. Thus, you say, "no" and you are seen as "the bad guy" by your child for a while. What can ease this, however, is to seek an alternative. When my sons were in the third or fourth grade, one of them was invited to an overnight birthday party of someone in their class at school. He was to bring his sleeping bag and they were going to "camp out" on the floor. My son was excited about going, but my wife and I were hesitant because we didn't know the boy or the home situation. After doing a little research, we felt that it was best that our son not go to the overnight birthday party. Of course, our son was upset and initially saw us as "the bad guys." We got his friend a gift and delivered it before the party began. Then we planned a special evening for both of our sons and when it came time to go to bed, my boys and I "camped out" on the den floor (I must admit that after they went to sleep, I got in the bed). Our son was quite content with how the evening went and wasn't as disappointed that he hadn't gone to the party. I will gladly be seen as "the bad guy" by my boys' friends or even by my boys themselves if it will protect them in some way. Doing this provides an atmosphere of security for your children.

The second example we saw of God carrying Israel was by providing for their physical needs. In America and within Christian families we would probably not think of this as much of a problem. It can be, though, in the following way. Did you notice that the emphasis was on God meeting Israel's needs and not their wants? Yes, there was a time in the wilderness that Israel complained about not having meat. God met their wants, but at the same time, because of Israel's greedy desires, He struck the people with a severe plague. What I am referring to here is the sin of materialism. I once read about the persecuted church in the Far East. The author pointed out that we, in America, face persecution also. No, it is not physical persecution like in the Far East, but it is the persecution of materialism. Trying to keep up with the modern trends in all aspects. You may have seen the bumper sticker, "He who dies with the most toys wins." Sadly, that depicts our society. It is amazing how much "stuff" adults and children alike accumulate over the years. And so often, we don't want to get rid of any of it even though we may have no need for it any longer and it may meet a need of someone less fortunate. And what is usually required to obtain all these possessions? Going into debt.

What did we see in Matthew 6 about the Father's care and provision for His children? He knows what we need. Well, parents are to do the same for their children. Please understand, I'm not saying it is wrong to have nice clothes, nice toys, etc. for our children. At the same time, however, we need to teach them the difference between needs and wants. We need to teach them that they don't necessarily need the designer name items. We need to teach them that going into debt is a form of bondage. We need to teach them that compared to the rest of the world, we, as Americans, are rich and thus, we should heed Paul's words as recorded in 1 Timothy 6:17-19. "Instruct those who are rich in this present world not to be conceited or to fix their hope on the uncertainty of riches, but on God, who richly supplies us with all things to enjoy. Instruct them to do good, to be rich in good works, to be generous and ready to share, storing up for themselves the treasure of a good foundation for the future, so that they may take hold of that which is life indeed." We need to teach them as Jesus taught in Luke 12:15b, "for not even when one has an abundance does his life consist of his possessions." We need to teach them that where their treasure is there will their heart be also. And as we treasure the kingdom of God and His righteousness, He will meet our needs as Matthew

6 informs us. That will provide a great deal of security for our children in that if they know God as their Father, even though all their possessions may be taken away, they are secure in that what is most important, they can never lose. You see, the important thing is not what they have, but who they have. As the writer of Psalm 73 learned, true prosperity is being continually with God and having His nearness as our good.

The third example we saw of God carrying Israel was through His laws and ordinances. Parents need to establish rules for their children. This is not only important for the purpose of establishing in your children acceptable behavior, but it is for their benefit. I heard of a father who told his small son, "Don't ever touch the eyes of the stove." You notice that the father did not mention not to touch the eyes of the stove only when they are on, but don't ever touch them, for if the son obeyed that rule, he would never get burned. Well, one day the little boy was near the stove and couldn't resist the temptation and touched one of the eyes of the stove. Unfortunately, this particular eye was on and he got burned. As the father was consoling his son, he told him that he had given the rule for his son's good. That is the reason why God gave His laws and ordinances to Israel. In Deuteronomy 6:24 Moses tells Israel, "So the LORD commanded us to observe all these statues, to fear the LORD our God for our good always and for our survival." This same thought is also stated in Deuteronomy 10:13. When parents establish rules for their children, it is for their good and survival and provides an atmosphere of security for them.

The final example we saw of God carrying Israel was in the patience He exhibited toward them. This is a vital lesson that parents need to learn. You see, we live in a society that seeks to hurry our children to grow up. Consequently, parents often expect them to act a certain way and if they don't, they are very impatient with them. How often do parents get upset with children when they have spilled something or broken something and it was unintentional? Then we, as parents, say something that demeans them in a certain way. How often have we told our small sons when they got hurt and start to cry, "Big boys don't cry." Dear parents, big boys do cry and the greatest example of this is, "Jesus wept." Children are going to mess up like parents do. Children are going to make stupid mistakes like parents do. Children aren't always going to act their age. A young girl once spilled some fingernail polish on the floor of an expensive house in which she lived with her parents. If that had occurred a couple of years earlier, she may have received a different reaction from her mother than she did. Her mother, however, had become a Christian and just said, "Let's hurry and clean it up." You see, the mother knew that her heavenly Father was patient with her and she was going to display that same patience toward her daughter. And what did the mother's patience display to her daughter? You are more important to me than a spill that may cause some damage to the floor. Her patience provided an atmosphere of security for her daughter.

We also saw, however, that God's patience did have a limit. Well, the same may be true for parents too. If our children become rebellious or could care less about the things of the Lord, there may come a time in which we have to let them go. This is what the father did with the prodigal son in Luke 15. No, this doesn't mean that we don't still love them or pray for them, but we establish a boundary where our patience has a limit. I have a friend who describes this as "putting them on the altar" and letting God deal with them.

So, God carried Israel in the wilderness as a man carries his son. When we, as parents, seek to imitate God and carry our children in a similar way, it will provide an atmosphere of security for them whereby they can grow and mature and be prepared to face life regardless of the difficulties.

Chapter Three

Being a Source of Comfort to Your Children

"As one whom his mother comforts,
so I will comfort you;"
—Isaiah 66:13a

Blessed be the God and Father of
our Lord Jesus Christ, the Father of
mercies and God of all comfort;
who comforts us in all our affliction
so that we may be able to comfort
those who are in any affliction with
the comfort with which we ourselves
are comforted by God. For just as
the sufferings of Christ are ours in
abundance, so also our comfort
is abundant through Christ.
—2 Corinthians 1:3-5

In Isaiah 66:10-14 God is giving a message to the exiles to encourage them. Several blessings are mentioned reference their glorious future. One of those blessings is that God will comfort them as a mother comforts her child. Then in 2 Corinthians 1:3-5,

Paul writes of the Christian being blessed by a comforting Father. Now, what usually is a requirement for a person receiving comfort? It is that they are experiencing some kind of pain, affliction, depression, suffering or other type of turmoil. Did Adam and Eve need any comfort in the Garden of Eden prior to their sin? Not according to Scripture. They had no problems. After their sin, however, they then began to experience painful circumstances for which they needed comfort. Even though God sought them out and preached the gospel to them (Genesis 3:15) and they believed, this did not isolate them from a life of difficulties and their need to be comforted.

One of the saddest things a Christian could ever do to a person with whom they are sharing the gospel of Jesus Christ is to tell them that if they become a Christian, life will be a bed of roses with no problems. Unfortunately, Christians are often taught that if they have enough faith, they will not experience any problems at all, to include financial or physical problems. What does such teaching basically reflect? A Christian should never be in need or in a situation to require comfort. Nothing could be further from the truth. Acts 14:22c says, "Through many tribulations we must enter the kingdom of God." And in Philippians 1:29 Paul writes, "For to you it has been granted for Christ's sake, not only to believe in Him, but also to suffer for His sake." As my Old Testament professor at RTS, Dr. Bruce Waltke, stated in a lecture, Jesus never said, "Follow Me for I have a wonderful plan for your life." Rather, He pointed them to a life of denying self and taking up the cross daily and following Him (Luke 9:23). In other words, He had them count the costs. So, suffering, tribulation and affliction are a part of the Christian life. Yet, how often do we feel like David as expressed in Psalm 69:20, "Reproach has broken my heart, and I am so sick. And I looked for sympathy, but there was none, And for comforters, but I found none." How then can we make it through such difficult times? We have a Father who is the source of comfort for us.

In 2 Corinthians 1:3 Paul blesses God because He is the Father of mercies and God of all comfort. The word "mercies" refers to pity or compassion for the cares or heartaches of others. And the word "comfort" means a calling to one's side or an exhortation or encouragement. It is used in Luke 2:25 when it speaks of Simeon who was looking for the consolation of Israel. This then refers to that which affords comfort or refreshment. In other words, the Messianic salvation. And what does the Messianic salvation point to? The cross. The cross is the basis for anyone receiving comfort from God the Father. As we've already seen from Ephesians 2:1-3, prior to our salvation, we were dead in our trespasses and sins and were by nature children of wrath. Thus, we were under a curse. We deserved the wrath of God. But, what did God do for us? He sent Jesus Christ to die on the cross for us and take the curse. As Paul wrote in Galatians 3:13, "Christ redeemed us from the curse of the Law, having become a curse for us—for it is written, 'CURSED IS EVERYONE WHO HANGS ON A TREE.'" And as 2 Corinthians 5:21 says, "He(God) made Him(Jesus) who knew no sin to be sin on our behalf, that we might become the righteousness of God in Him." Thus, we are clothed in His righteousness and could now experience the comfort that only God could give. Consequently, as Romans 8:31b-32 tells us, "...If God is for us, who is against us? He who did not spare His own Son, but delivered Him up for us all, how will He not also with Him freely give us all things?"

So, as a child of God, we need not view Him as a Judge, but as a Father who freely gives us all things. And one of the things He gives to His children is His comfort. Therefore, the cross is the basis for God's children experiencing His comfort. Truly then, He is worthy of blessing and praise.

Well, what is the comfort we receive from our Father? Second Corinthians 1:4a,5 tell us. Let's focus on verse 5 first. Verse 5a reiterates a little of what we've already mentioned. We can expect to suffer as Christians. The word "suffer" speaks of a calamity or evil that a person might experience. In this case it refers to a calamity or evil we experience as a result of being a follower of Christ. Paul knew this quite well in his own life. In 1 Corinthians 4:10, he mentions that he was a fool for Christ's sake and then he records all that he had faced. He received no honor, but suffered hunger, thirst and was roughly treated, just to name a few. Then in 2 Corinthians 11:24-27, Paul also mentions his beatings, lashes, dangers, labors, and hardships. Paul was not the only New Testament writer that knew of the reality of suffering as a follower of Christ. Peter wrote in 1 Peter 4:12, "Beloved, do not be surprised at the fiery ordeal among you, which comes upon you for your testing, as though some strange thing were happening to you." So, the sufferings of being a follower of Christ are ours in abundance and the word "abundance" means to overflow. This word is used of a flower going from a bud to full bloom.

Thankfully, though, verse 5 has two parts to it. In this verse Paul is making a comparison. It is a comparison between the sufferings of Christ, which are ours in abundance with our comfort, which is also abundant through Christ. In other words, in the midst of his sufferings, Paul received overflowing comfort, encouragement, and refreshment from his heavenly Father which enabled him to bear the sufferings.

Thus, Paul had experienced the truth of verse 4a that our Father comforts us in all our affliction. The word "affliction" is a word which means a pressing, a pressure or an oppression. It refers to anything which burdens the spirit. And these sufferings and afflictions have both an external and internal dimension. Regardless, our Father is there to comfort us. Now, as we think of Him being there to comfort us in all our afflictions, there are two main truths to consider: Why He can comfort and then the means He uses to comfort.

Let's begin by considering why He can comfort. He can comfort us, first of all, because He is sovereign and omniscient. Have you ever experienced an affliction and in the midst of it said, "Father God, why don't You do something about this? Can't You see that I'm hurting?" Yes. He sees it very well for as we saw previously in Isaiah 63:9a, God says, "In all their (our) affliction He was afflicted..." And in Zechariah 2:8 we saw, "for he who touches you, touches the apple of His eye."

Well, why doesn't He do something about it? There are times that He does immediately intervene. I'm sure that all of us have experienced occasions where God has quickly intervened to help us out when facing a difficult circumstance or suffering or affliction. For example, when our family first moved to Orlando, Florida, we made a decision on a place to live that really wasn't a wise decision. God, our gracious Father, intervened and the loan fell through which meant that we got our deposit back and were then able to purchase a house that better met our needs.

Then there are times when it may appear that our Father doesn't do anything to help us or is very slow in helping us. Why? Of course, it's not because He is not able to bring it to an end, but as Romans 8:28-29 tells us, He is working and causing our difficult situations to work together for our good as He is conforming us into the image of Christ. There are many promises from Scripture that we could claim which reference this, but I want to share three of them with you. The Psalmist writes in Psalm 84:11, "For the LORD God is a sun and shield; The LORD gives grace and glory; No good thing does He withhold from those who walk uprightly." You see then, from our Father's omniscient perspective, the affliction or difficulty is a good thing. Writing to the exiles in Babylon, the LORD promises in Jeremiah 29:11, "For I know the plans that I have for you...plans for welfare and not for calamity to give you a future and a hope." And then speaking of our Father's sovereign control over our lives, David writes in Psalm 37:23-24, "The steps of a man are established by the LORD; And He delights in his way. When he falls, he shall not be hurled headlong; Because the LORD is the One who holds his hand." Did you notice that our difficulty, affliction or suffering has been established or ordained by our Father and He delights in our way, whatever we face? Thus, as we saw in the previous chapter, we should not complain about what our sovereign, loving Father has ordained for us to experience. But please realize, whatever affliction we face, from our sovereign Father's omniscient perspective, it is not designed to destroy us, but to develop us to give us a future and a hope. Think of our

Father's relationship with His perfect Son, Jesus Christ. In Hebrews 5:8 we learn that, "Although He was a Son, He learned obedience from the things which He suffered." If there was ever a person that didn't need to or shouldn't have suffered any affliction at all, it was Jesus. Yet, He did and the Father didn't remove the suffering or affliction. Why? Because through it, Jesus learned obedience. The same is true for us.

This points to another reason why our Father can comfort His children. He, through Jesus Christ, has experienced all temptations, afflictions, and sufferings that we could ever face. This great truth is demonstrated in Hebrews especially. Hebrews 2:18 tells us, "For since He Himself was tempted in that which He has suffered, He is able to come to the aid of those who are tempted." And Hebrews 4:15-16 states, "For we do not have a high priest who cannot sympathize with our weaknesses, but One who has been tempted in all things as we are, yet without sin. Let us therefore draw near with confidence to the throne of grace, that we may receive mercy and may find grace to help in time of need." Now, I've heard some people question how serious Jesus' temptations really were. After all, He could not have sinned. So, since He couldn't sin, was His temptation that bad? It was much more severe than we could ever imagine. It was because He couldn't sin that His temptations were so extreme and severe. When I examine my own life, I so often submit to temptation and sin even before the temptation gets really bad. Jesus, however, experienced temptation to its fullest and still didn't sin. And the same could be said of the afflictions, sufferings, and trials that He experienced. He experienced them to the utmost degree. Just think of Gethsemane. Luke records He was in such agony that He fervently prayed and His sweat became like drops of blood falling down upon the ground (Luke 22:44). And when He returned to heaven, He took His humanity with Him and as we saw in the Hebrews passages, He understands all that we face. Thus, our Father can comfort us because He is sovereign and omniscient and He knows what we experience because Jesus has experienced every type of affliction we will ever face.

The question now arises, how does the Father comfort His children? Here again, it may seem that the Father doesn't intervene too quickly in most of our afflictions, but allows us to go through them for various lengths of time. Even so, in the midst of the afflictions, His comfort is ours in abundance. In the Isaiah 66 passage we really see the heart behind the Father's comfort. His comfort is compared to a mother's comfort. When a very young child gets hurt or needs comfort, to whom does he usually go to? His mother. W. Clarkson wrote, "It is the province of the teacher to instruct, of the father to direct, of the elder brother to lead, and of the mother to console. She is the comforter of the troubled heart."[1] Well, how does a mother comfort? Clarkson mentions three ways: tenderly in that she is gracious and considerate; unfailingly in that no child feels that the number of times he has come before is any reason to doubt the welcome he will receive if he comes again; and effectually in that the mother knows what way to comfort-in silence, speech or by action.[2]

From the Father's heart of comfort then flows the means by which He brings comfort in the midst of our afflictions. I want to examine several means that He uses to bring comfort to His children. First, He comforts us through His Holy Spirit. Previously we read Psalm 69:20 which really was a prophecy pointing to Jesus. There were no comforters for Him. As Matthew recorded, when Jesus was arrested, "all the disciples left Him and fled" (Matthew 26:56). Charles Spurgeon wrote, "His dearest ones had sought their own safety, and left their Lord alone. A sick man needs comforters, and a persecuted man needs sympathy; but our blessed Surety found neither on that dark and doleful night when the power of darkness had their hour. A spirit like that of our Lord feels acutely desertion by beloved and trusted friends, and yearns for real sympathy."[3] And think of His experience upon the cross. As He was bearing God's wrath for our sin, He cried out, "MY GOD, MY GOD, WHY HAST THOU FORSAKEN ME?" (Matthew 27:46). Truly, there were no comforters for Jesus at that time. That is never true for a child of God, however. And it is because of Jesus' death on the cross, where there were no comforters, that we can claim the promise of our Father's comfort.

In John's gospel, chapters 14-16 have been described as Jesus' last will and testament to His followers. In other words, what He was leaving His followers after His death. In John 14:16-18 He stated, "And I will ask the Father, and He will give you another Helper, that He may be with you forever; that is the Spirit of truth...I will not leave you as orphans." What do you think of when you hear the word "orphan"? A child who has no parents. That is never a concern for the child of God. We see that the Father will give His children another Helper of the same kind and the word "Helper" is the word "paracletos" which means one called alongside to help. In fact, in John 16:7 Jesus tells His disciples that it was to their advantage that He go away whereby He would send the Helper to them. Yes, this brought sadness to His disciples, but as a man Jesus could only be at one place at one time. And soon He would be sending them throughout the world and with the coming of the Holy Spirit they all could be comforted as He came alongside them in the midst of the afflictions they faced. Our Father has children in every area of the world and all of us have His Holy Spirit whereby we will never be alone and feel like an orphan and thus, experience comfort through His presence.

Second, our Father comforts us through His word. The longest chapter in the Bible, Psalm 119, deals extensively with God's word and in it we are told of the comfort it brings. For example, in Psalm 119:50,52,92-93 we read: "This is my comfort in my affliction, That Thy word has revived me...I have remembered Thine ordinances from of old, O LORD, And comfort myself...If Thy law had not been my delight, Then I would have perished in my affliction. I will never forget Thy precepts, For by them Thou hast revived me." How many times has the Holy Spirit brought to your heart a Scripture which has comforted you? How many times has a friend shared with you a Scripture in the midst of affliction, and it's brought comfort? And what is the nature of God's word that so often brings such great comfort? It is His promises. One promise that should always bring comfort to His children is that He will never place more on us than we can bear by His grace. You may remember Paul's thorn in the flesh as recorded in 2 Corinthians 12. He asked three times that the Lord take it away, but the Lord's answer was "no." That, however, was not the only answer that He gave Paul. He told Paul in 2 Corinthians 12:9, "My grace is sufficient for you, for power is perfected in weakness." That word from the Lord, His promise, brought such comfort to Paul, which resulted in his saying, "Most gladly, therefore, I will rather boast about my weaknesses, that the power of Christ may dwell in me."

Third, our Father comforts us through prayer. In Philippians 4:6-7 Paul writes, "Be anxious for nothing, but in everything by prayer and supplication with thanksgiving let your requests be made known to God. And the peace of God, which surpasses all comprehension, shall guard your hearts and minds in Christ Jesus." This aspect of comfort really speaks of the Father's care for His children in that we can communicate openly with Him. We can tell Him that we don't understand. We can cast all our cares or anxieties upon Him because He cares for us as 1 Peter 5:7 tells us. But as Philippians 4:6 also tells us, we are to do this with a thankful heart trusting His sovereign control over our lives.

Fourth, our Father comforts us through other people. It appears from 2 Corinthians that there were times that Paul battled depression. And God his Father brought him comfort through fellow saints. In 2 Corinthians 7:6-7 Paul wrote, "But God, who comforts the depressed, comforted us by the coming of Titus; and not only by his coming, but also by the comfort with which he was comforted in you, as he reported to us your longing, your mourning, your zeal for me; so that I rejoiced even more." And many times that comfort is just a person's presence and silence. We recall the great afflictions that Job experienced. Initially, Job's three friends came and sat with him for seven days and nights without speaking a word as they saw that his pain was very great (Job 2:13). I believe they were a real comfort to him when they were silent. It was when they began to speak, however, that they failed to bring comfort. Why? It was because they weren't handling accurately God's word related to Job's situation. In fact, Job calls his friends, "sorry comforters" and states that they were tormenting and crushing him with words (Job 16:1; 19:2). Job had quite a different experience from the apostle Paul.

So, the Father is truly a source of comfort to His children in the midst of our affliction and parents are to be the same for their children whom God has entrusted to them. We saw previously of ways in which a mother comforts based on the passage in Isaiah 66. Yet, it appears that in our society many parents are missing out on the blessing of being a source of comfort to their children. Let's recall Psalm 69:20b, "And I looked for sympathy, but there was none." Charles Stanford wrote, "Even under ordinary circumstances we yearn for sympathy. Without it, the heart will contract and droop, and shut like a flower in an unkindly atmosphere, but it will open again amidst the sounds of frankness and the scenes of love. When we are in trouble, this want is in proportion still more pressing; and, for the sorrowful heart to feel alone, is a grief greater than nature can sustain. A glance of sympathy seems to help it more than the gift of untold riches; and a loving look, even from a little child who is sorry for us, or a simple word from some homely friend, will sometimes brace the spirit to new exertions, and seem almost to waken life within the grasp of death."[4] Stanford wrote these words in 1859. How much more do we need to hear them today, and especially for parents to be that for their children. We must realize that it is not only the parents' responsibility to be a source of comfort to our children, but it is also a real blessing. And we must never forget, when our children are in pain, regardless of the cause, they are going to seek comfort in some way to alleviate it. It may be drugs, alcohol, an illicit relationship or, sadly, even suicide, but they are going to try to find some comfort. Yes, as very young children, they will naturally go to their parents, especially their mothers, for comfort, but as they grow older that will not necessarily be the case. Parents are to provide an atmosphere whereby their children will always desire to come to them as a source of comfort rather than seeking comfort from those sources that may be destructive to them. Here again, there are no perfect parents, but there are ways that we can provide comfort for our children to demonstrate to them how much we care, just as our heavenly Father perfectly provides comfort for His children. The best way for parents to provide comfort is just by being there for their children. Now we will address our presence with our children or spending time with them in more detail in the next chapter, but this really speaks of those ways we can be there to be a source of comfort to our children. We read previously Jesus' words that He would not leave us as orphans. Too often it's possible that children can feel like orphans even in a family with parents. The parents are not there to provide the support the children need.

Just as with our heavenly Father, there are times when parents can directly intervene in their children's affliction and bring it to an end which brings comfort to the child. In so many cases, however, the parent may not be able to prevent or stop the affliction. This may be for one of two reasons. First, due to the nature of the affliction, you may not be able to do anything about it. Second, you may not do anything about the affliction even if you could because you know it is for your child's growth in that they need to experience what they are going through. I read a beautiful illustration of this truth reference a butterfly. A man found a cocoon of a butterfly. One day he noticed a small opening appear and watched the butterfly for several hours as it struggled to force its body through the little hole. Then it seemed to stop making progress. It seemed as if the butterfly had gotten as far as it could and could go no further. Thus, the man decided to help the butterfly. He got a pair of scissors and cut off the remaining part of the cocoon. Of course, the butterfly was able to easily emerge from the cocoon. The butterfly, however, had a swollen body and small, shriveled wings. The man thought at any moment the wings would expand and support the body which would contract at any time. This never happened though. Sadly, the butterfly spent the rest of its life crawling around with a swollen body and shriveled wings.

It was never able to fly. The man thought he was being kind to the butterfly in its apparent affliction. He did not realize, however, that the butterfly's struggle to get out of the cocoon was God's way of forcing fluid from the butterfly's body into its wings so that it could fly. This relates back to what we learned about our sovereign Father earlier in the chapter. He knows the type of afflictions and struggles we need in our lives whereby we can grow. If He didn't ordain for us to experience any afflictions, it would cripple us. We could never fly, you may say, for His glory.

Parents need to learn this same truth. There may be some afflictions that we could prevent our children from going through or alleviate once they're in them. These afflictions may have been a result of some wrong choices or bad decisions. By allowing them to go through these afflictions, hopefully they will grow from them. Still, however, parents will hurt for their children in the midst of what they are facing. No, we may not alleviate the affliction, even if we could, but we surely need to be there to be a source of comfort for them. And this comfort can take on various forms just as we saw previously with our Father being a source of comfort to His children.

We can comfort our children with our words. When I was in college, the heavenly Father allowed me the privilege of playing football. I was a place kicker. When I was a sophomore the number one place kicker was hurt. Since there were no other place kickers on the team, I was better than nothing to handle the kicking responsibilities. The heavenly Father was gracious to me as I did fairly well the first few games. About mid-season, the number one place kicker had recovered from his injury. So, the next game, which was a road trip, the coaches decided to take him rather than me. I was devastated. As quickly as I could after practice, I called my parents and just hearing their voice and words brought such comfort. And part of their words that brought comfort was from God's word, Romans 8:28.

Then we can comfort our children just by being there and not really saying anything, but listening. A couple of years after I graduated from college, my wife and I went to visit my parents for the weekend. I have a brother who is seven years younger than I who still was a teenager at that time. This particular weekend he was experiencing a difficult time in a relationship. After supper, he went to his room and our mother went to be with him. She was with him for quite a while and when she came back to the family room where we were, she apologized for being gone so long, especially since we had just come home. She did not need to apologize. She was doing exactly what she was supposed to do. She was hurting for her son and even though she could not remove the affliction, she was there to bring comfort by her presence. And I'm sure she didn't say much, but just listened and expressed her love.

There is one final way that we can bring comfort to our children in affliction. We can allow our children to be totally honest with us in their communication. In other words, not be condemning towards them regardless of their actions. Earlier in this chapter we focused on Jesus as our great High Priest from Hebrews 4:15-16. We saw that because of Him we can come to the throne of grace with confidence to receive mercy and find grace to help in time of need. How often do we, as the heavenly Father's children, come to Him suffering afflictions because we have sinned or made bad choices. Yet, we come to Him through Jesus to receive mercy and grace to help in our time of need. Parents, can your children come to you with any problem and expect to receive the comfort of mercy and grace to help in their time of need? Several years ago, a teenage girl was preparing a paper for school. In her research she found out that on a percentage basis, more Christian girls who get pregnant out of wedlock get abortions than non-Christian girls. How can that be? Could it be that they fear being condemned by their parents for having embarrassed their parents rather than expecting mercy and grace? I've heard of parents getting upset over their children's behavior because of how it will make the parent look before their friends rather than a concern for their children. If the children know that their parents feel this way, you can almost be certain that they will not communicate with them when they face an affliction because of bad choices or sin. And as stated earlier, chances are they will seek comfort from another source, which may make the affliction even worse. In the example just described, it was getting an abortion, which could be made worse in later years through guilt and also physical repercussions.

Afflictions are a part of life in this sinful world. They are not a respecter of persons or age. Parents, though, have the tremendous privilege and blessing of being a source of comfort to their children in their afflictions. And as we carry out this privilege and blessing, we will hopefully be reflecting to them a loving Father who is a perfect source of comfort. Hadn't you rather they come to you, who can direct them to our Father rather than their seeking comfort from worldly and evil sources?

Chapter Four

Being There for Your Children

> "Ask, and it shall be given to you; seek, and
> you shall find; knock, and it shall be opened to you.
> For everyone who asks receives, and he who seeks
> finds, and to him who knocks it shall be opened.
> Or what man is there among you, when his son shall
> ask him for a loaf, will give him a stone? Or if he
> shall ask for a fish, he will not give him a snake,
> will he? If you then, being evil, know how to give
> good gifts to your children, how much more shall
> your Father who is in heaven give what is good
> to those who ask Him!"
> —Matthew 7:7-11

The passage of Scripture that is the basis for this chapter comes from Jesus' Sermon on the Mount and contains two verses, Matthew 7:7-8, that have been memorized by numerous Christians. These verses are such an encouragement in that they inform us that we can come to our heavenly Father in prayer for guidance. Every child of God is on a spiritual journey or pilgrimage. This journey for each of us is similar to Abraham's journey as recorded in Hebrews 11:8, "By faith Abraham, when he was called, obeyed by going out to a place which he was to receive for an inheritance; and he went out, not knowing where he was going." As one Puritan stated, "Abraham went out, not knowing where he went; but he did know with Whom he went."[1] In other words, he did not know the challenges he would face but he trusted God for divine guidance. The same is true for each of His children. In our journey toward our eternal inheritance, we are going to face many challenges that we are unaware of. It is such a blessing to know that we can go to our Father any time in prayer for divine guidance. Jewish Rabbis stated, "God is as near to His creatures, as the ear to the mouth. Human beings can hardly hear two people talking at once, but God, if all the world calls to Him at one time, hears their cry."[2] I think that most parents can understand this on the natural level. Parent, if your child is in a group of children all making noise and your child screams out or cries, can't you distinguish his cry or voice from the other children? Of course you can. That is how it is with our heavenly Father. When we come to Him in prayer, He can always distinguish us as one of His children coming for guidance.

Matthew 7:7-8 emphasizes the two sides of prayer: the human side and the divine side. Notice first the human side. In both verses the child of God asks, seeks, and knocks. Each of these verbs is in the present tense and speaks of a continuous action. Let's examine them more closely. The word "asks" refers to a petition made by one who is lesser in position than the one to whom the petition is made. In Scripture, whenever we see Jesus asking of the Father in prayer, the Greek word always refers to the one making the petition being on an equal status with the one to whom the petition is made. Thus, it is God asking God. Here though, it speaks of a child asking his heavenly Father. In this asking there is to be humility and a real yearning of the heart.[3] This attitude is depicted in a very familiar parable of Jesus as recorded in Luke 18. It is the Parable of the Pharisee and the Tax-gatherer. Two men went to the temple to pray, a Pharisee and a tax-gatherer. If you examine the Pharisee's prayer, you will notice that he didn't ask anything. Rather, Jesus stated that he was praying to himself and his prayer focused on his self-righteousness as shown by him stating how much better he was than other people, especially the tax-gatherer. The tax-gatherer, on the other hand, humbly asked for God's mercy. His asking spoke of a real need and that is the emphasis of the asking in Matthew 7:7-8—knowing our need and asking our Father Who will supply.

Then Jesus teaches that we are to continuously "seek." This seeking speaks of asking plus acting.[4] If we want to understand what it means to seek we need to look at the life of Jesus. A beautiful verse that describes Jesus seeking is Luke 19:10, "For the Son of Man has come to seek and to save that which was lost. To what extent did Jesus seek the lost? To the extent of ridicule by His own family and the Pharisees who described Him as a friend of sinners. To the extent of being called a blasphemer and even having His works accredited to the power of Satan. To the extent of being nailed to a cross and yet praying, "Father forgive them." To the extent of saving a thief on the cross beside Him even though He was in such agony. That describes the diligent seeking of Jesus. When we pray we are to seek with a similar type diligence. Such is depicted in Psalm 27:8 when David said, "When Thou didst say, 'Seek My face,' my heart said to Thee, 'Thy face, O LORD, I shall seek.'"

Finally, we are to continuously "knock." This continuous knocking speaks of asking plus acting plus persevering.[5] In other words, persistence. Such a persistence is shown by Jacob in Genesis 32 when he wrestled with the Lord. Genesis 32:26 records, "Then he (Lord) said, 'Let me go, for the dawn is breaking.' But he (Jacob) said, 'I will not let you go unless you bless me.'" And Jesus taught several parables on persistence in prayer. Of course, this persistence does not speak of making a blanket request for anything I want. Rather, it speaks of a persistence in praying according to our Father's will (1 John 5:14-15). Another way of saying this is that we will pray for those things that Jesus would pray for.

Then there is the divine side of prayer. It is that our heavenly Father will answer. We shall receive. We shall find and it shall be opened to us. So, Christians have the great privilege of praying and knowing that our Father longs to answer and meet our needs.

To further illustrate this great truth, Jesus makes a contrast between an earthly father giving to his children with the heavenly Father giving to His children. He asks two questions in verses 9-10. The first question involves a son asking his father for a loaf and Jesus asks, *will that father give his son a stone instead?* Such a question may seem strange to us, but in this region there were many stones that looked like a small loaf of bread.[6] Then in verse 10, the second question involves a son asking his father for a fish. Surely the father would not give him a snake, would he? This snake may have been a water snake and could very well have referred to an eel which according to Leviticus 11:12 could not be eaten, for it was unclean.[7] The parallel passage to this passage in Matthew 7 is in Luke 11, which gives another contrast. In Luke 11:12 Jesus states that if a son asked his father for an egg, the father would not give him a scorpion, would he? As with the other two examples, a scorpion in a certain position can look like an egg.[8] Of course, in all three of Jesus' questions, He is expecting a "no" answer. So, what is Jesus trying to tell us? In each of the three examples, He is pointing to the fact that an earthly father would not deceive his son by giving him something that would be dangerous when he had asked for something good.

In Matthew 7:11 then, Jesus emphasizes the contrast. If earthly fathers, who are evil, know how to give good gifts to their children, then how much more will our heavenly Father give what is good to His children who ask Him. What is Jesus saying here? First of all, let's realize what He is not saying. When He refers to earthly fathers as being evil, He is not referring to those fathers who are truly evil and physically abuse their children even to the point of death. Rather, He is talking about good earthly fathers. Regardless of how good an earthly father is, all fathers have a tendency to do evil. Gardiner Spring, a Puritan who pastored Brick Presbyterian Church in New York City for 62 years, wrote, "There is great imperfection in earthly parents compared with God. Earthly parents know not how to adapt their bounty at all times to the wants of their children. They give when they ought not to give, and withhold when they ought not to withhold."[9] Still though, they seek to give good gifts to their children. Now, if that is true with earthly fathers, how much more is it true of our perfect heavenly Father. He will only give what is good to His children who ask Him. It is impossible for Him to give His children anything that is evil.

Joseph knew the reality of this great truth. I briefly mentioned in chapter 1 that his brothers hated him and this resulted in their selling him into slavery. What happened then? He was taken to Egypt and eventually put in jail for something he didn't do. This later resulted in his interpreting a dream of Pharaoh concerning seven years of plenty followed by seven years of famine. Pharaoh put him in charge to oversee the years of plenty so that they could survive during the famine. The famine was so severe that eventually his brothers were sent by their father to get grain. On their second trip to Egypt, Joseph revealed himself to them, which ultimately led to his whole family moving down to Egypt. When Joseph's father, Jacob, died, his brothers were fearful that Joseph would seek revenge. He told them, however, "Do not be afraid, for am I in God's place? And as for you, you meant evil against me, but God meant it for good in order to bring about this present result, to preserve many people alive" (Genesis 50:19-20). Joseph recognized that all he had experienced had come from his heavenly Father, who could never do evil to His children, but only good.

So, Jesus teaches that our heavenly Father gives what is good to His children who ask Him. Now we need to focus on what is the good that He gives. We know from James 1 that He is the giver of every good and perfect gift. Of course, that refers to all that He gives His children, but there is one particular aspect that we need to consider. It also comes from the parallel passage in Luke 11. In Luke 11:13, the good that the Father gives is the Holy Spirit to those who ask Him. Do you see the importance of this? It is that the Father longs to give His presence through His Holy Spirit to His children. Let's make sure we understand what Jesus is referring to.

We know that when a person becomes a Christian, the Holy Spirit comes to indwell them. Jesus is not talking about the permanent indwelling of the Holy Spirit. He also is not talking about the truth of God's omnipresence. As David wrote in Psalm 139:7-8, we cannot go anywhere from His Spirit and we cannot flee from His presence. If we ascend to heaven, He is there or if we make our bed in Sheol, behold He is there also. Rather, He is talking about the filling of the Holy Spirit as Ephesians 5:18 tells us in which we are empowered to live for His glory by displaying His fruit in our lives. To put it in the words of this chapter's title, our heavenly Father longs to be there for His children. He longs for His children to experience the intimacy of His presence in their lives whereby they can live an abundant, fruitful life for His glory.

There are examples in the Scriptures of saints experiencing and realizing the importance of God's presence in their lives. I want to focus on two Old Testament examples that I briefly mentioned in chapter 2, but now want to expand further to emphasize this great truth. The first example deals with Moses leading Israel through the wilderness. God's promise to Israel was that He would bring about their deliverance from Egyptian bondage and take them to a land flowing with milk and honey. After their release from bondage, we are familiar with Israel's disobedience of making the golden calf and worshiping it as Moses was on Mount Sinai receiving the law. Moses intercedes for the people and God tells him to go lead the people where He had told him, but He would punish them for their sin. In Exodus 33 we read of Israel resuming their journey toward the Promised Land at God's direction. In verses 2-3, God tells Moses, "And I will send an angel before you and I will drive out the Canaanite, the Amorite, the Hittite, the Perizzite, the Hivite and the Jebusite. Go up to a land flowing with milk and honey; for I will not go up in your midst, because you are an obstinate people, lest I destroy you on the way." This saddened the people and they went into mourning. Moses again intercedes for the people. Moses' intercession is found in verses 12-13: "See, Thou dost say to me, 'Bring up this people!' But Thou Thyself hast not let me know whom Thou wilt send with me. Moreover, Thou hast said, 'I have known you by name, and you have also found favor in My sight.' Now therefore, I pray Thee, if I have found favor in Thy sight, let me know Thy ways, that I might know Thee, so that I may find favor in Thy sight. Consider too, that this nation is Thy people." Then God told Moses, "My presence shall go with you, and I will give you rest" (v. 14) to which Moses responded, "If Thy presence does not go with us, do not lead us up from here" (v. 15). Did you notice the significance of this? Even though Israel was an obstinate people, God was still going to give them the land that flowed with milk and honey. Only He was going to send an angel before them rather than going up Himself. What then was the basis for Moses' intercession? It was that the land meant nothing, even though it was plenteous, if God's presence was not with them.

Another example of a saint realizing the importance of God's presence in his life was Asaph as recorded in Psalm 73. Asaph knew that God was good to Israel and to those who were pure in heart, but he was facing a difficult time. In fact, he stated that his feet came close to stumbling and his steps had almost slipped as he was envious of the arrogant and as he saw the prosperity of the wicked. Then he contrasted the life of the wicked versus his righteous life. The wicked seemed to have it so easy while he felt that he had been stricken all day long and chastened every morning. As he tried to understand this, it was troublesome to him until he came to the sanctuary of God. It was there that he realized two important truths. First, he perceived the end of the wicked. God set them in slippery places. He also will cast them down to destruction and destroy them in a moment as they are utterly swept away by sudden terrors. In other words, what ease the wicked do experience is for this life only and thus, is like a vapor compared to eternity. But there was a second truth that he realized that was so much more important. He realized that he was continually with God Who had taken hold of his right hand and would guide him with His counsel and afterward receive him to glory. Thus, Asaph could say, "Whom have I in heaven but Thee? And besides Thee, I desire nothing on earth...But as for me, the nearness of God is my good" (v.25,28a). Asaph had started out the Psalm by stating that God is good to those who are pure in heart and he closes out the Psalm by emphasizing the good is the nearness of God. In other words, the good is God's presence for his children.

This great truth is also illustrated in the New Testament by the author of Hebrews. In Hebrews 13:5 he writes, "Let your character be free from the love of money, being content with what you have; for He Himself has said, 'I WILL NEVER DESERT YOU, NOR WILL I EVER FORSAKE YOU.'" Of course, this passage does not teach that having money is evil, but it is the love of money that is evil, as 1 Timothy 6:10 tells us. Christians, however, are to be content with what we have. Let me ask you, "What do you have?" If you immediately focus on your bank account, retirement account or possessions, you are focusing on the wrong area. True contentment comes in experiencing our Father's presence. Haddon W. Robinson wrote, "If you have everything else but the Lord, you don't have much at all. If you have the Lord's presence and little else, you can be content. Better to have a satisfied soul than a thick wallet."[10] I think the prophet Habakkuk's words summarize this thought very well when he wrote, "Though the fig tree should not blossom, And there be no fruit on the vines, Though the yield of the olive should fail, And the fields produce no food, Though the flock should be cut off from the fold, And there be no cattle in the stalls, Yet I will exult in the LORD, I will rejoice in the God of my salvation" (Habakkuk 3:17-18). What was he saying? Even though all the circumstances of life may be against me, I can rejoice because I am experiencing God's presence through His great salvation. Here again, it is not what you have, but Who you have.

Moses, Asaph and the writer of Hebrews are not the only ones who have known the importance of God's presence. Saints throughout the history of the church have been comforted by His presence in their lives. Brother Lawrence was a 17th century monk who was known for sensing God's presence even in a monastery kitchen. In fact, he spoke of being "known of God and caressed by Him."

Near the end of his life, Hudson Taylor, the pioneer missionary to China wrote, "I am so weak that I cannot work; I cannot read my Bible; I cannot even pray. I can only lie still in God's arms like a child, and trust."[11] But this great truth of God's presence can be understood by even the youngest of children. Joanie Yoder wrote of a friend who overheard a conversation between her two grandchildren. The five-year-old grandson said, "I talk to Jesus in my head!" The three-year-old granddaughter responded, "I don't—I just cuddle with Him!"[12]

Our heavenly Father longs to be there for us and for us to experience His presence more than we long for it. This was depicted to me personally several years ago in a very practical way. I was taking a trip which required me being at the airport very early. If I was to have a quiet time with my heavenly Father, it would mean that I would have to get up a lot earlier than normal. I wanted to have the time with Him before I started my trip, but I didn't know if I would really be able to wake up and be alert at such an early hour. So, before I went to bed I prayed to my Father that He would wake me whereby I could have that time with Him. When the alarm went off the next morning at that early hour, I immediately awoke and was very alert, in fact, more alert than usual when I would sleep a little later. That experience really spoke to my heart in that my Father longed for me to spend time with Him. I'm not the only one who has had such an experience. Others have told me of similar type experiences.

Child of God, we have a Father who longs to be there for His children through His presence. Parents, how vital it is that we imitate our Father and do the same for our children. This is especially true in our society when lives are so busy and families are pulled in so many directions. Parents must be willing to make sacrifices and deny some of their desires in order to be there for their children. By doing this we demonstrate to them how important they are to us. I want to emphasize three practical ways that we can demonstrate to our children how important they are through our presence and being there for them.

The first area to consider is the actual amount of time we spend with our children. We often hear the statement that it is not the quantity of time that we spend with our children, but the quality of time. We must realize, however, that most children, especially our younger children, don't differentiate between the two. To them, the quantity of time equals the quality of time. This became evident to me several years ago when my sons were playing T-ball. The parents of one of their teammates often would not attend the games because they conflicted with their bowling league. I felt so sorry for that young boy. Were his parents' actions saying that their bowling league was more important to them than being at his game? I must admit, however, that I learned the importance of this lesson a few years earlier the hard way. I was in seminary and one evening I was studying in the bedroom of our apartment while the boys were in the den with their mother. The boys were a little over two years old. One of them asked their mother where I was and she stated I was studying. Then he responded, "Daddy, too busy." I heard that and immediately put down my books and went in the den to be with them. From that point on I tried not to study until after they went to bed. Of course, there are times when we will be hindered from being with our children at certain activities or events, but that should be the exception rather than the rule. I remember hearing Josh McDowell once talk about a particular activity he did with his children. As you probably know, Josh travels a lot because of his ministry, but when he was home, his children knew they were a priority. He had a routine that he would do with them prior to their going to bed. Even if there were guests over at their house visiting, Josh would excuse himself for a period of time so that he could follow the routine with his children. What was Josh doing? He was letting his children know how important it was for him to spend time with them.

G. Campbell Morgan told a story of a father and young daughter who were great friends and loved to be in each other's presence. The father, however, began to notice a change in his daughter. If he went on a walk, rather than going with him as before, she excused herself. He grieved over this loss of time together and couldn't understand what was going on. At his next birthday, his daughter gave him a pair of exquisitely crafted slippers and said, "I have made them for you." He now realized why his daughter had spent less time with him the last three months. He then told her, "My darling, I like these slippers very much, but next time buy the slippers and let me have you all the days. I would rather have my child than anything she can make for me."[13] Previously, concerning our heavenly Father's presence, we focused on the fact that it is not what we have but who we have that is important. That is exactly what that father was saying to his daughter. I would much rather have your presence than anything you may do for me.

As young adults, my sons occasionally played on a softball team at a local park. Their mother and I would still try to attend every game that they played. Do you know why I have done that throughout the years? Of course I want to be near them, but it is also because I was taught the importance of this by my parents who were always there for me. I started playing football in junior high school in Paducah, Kentucky. My parents came to every game. In my ninth grade year, they organized a banquet for the football team after the season and my dad was the Master of Ceremonies. Prior to entering high school, we moved to Chattanooga, Tennessee. I played football for three years and my dad came to every practice possible. He worked shift work so that when he worked the 3-11 PM shift he was unable to attend. But when he was scheduled to work that shift and we had a game, he would always switch with someone else so that he and my mother could attend.

After graduating from high school, I went to a college in the northeast about 800 miles from home. Still, my parents came to as many games as possible. Whenever they were unable to attend a game, I would call them as soon as possible to tell them what had happened. Often they would drive all night to attend one of my games. I remember my junior year that they came to a home game and then the very next week they drove about 800 miles in the opposite direction from Chattanooga with my aunt and uncle to attend an away game. As I've already mentioned, the only position I played in college was a place kicker and my team was not known for scoring a lot of points. So, my parents came and drove all those miles knowing that I might only be involved in one play, the kickoff. They still came, however. It was important for them to be there for me and it was important for me to have them there.

There was another very special way that my parents were there for me while in college. Every Thursday I could expect to receive a coffee can of homemade "blonde brownies", one of my favorites. My mother would make them on Monday mornings and my dad would get them in the mail that same day so that they would arrive on Thursday. I would love to know how many brownies my mother made during that four-year period. The brownies were so popular that many of my classmates were close by when I opened the can. In fact, there were some occasions when they opened the can even before I got to them. Being so far from home was tough, but those brownies were a constant reminder that my parents were there for me. And they have continued to demonstrate that throughout the years.

A second practical way of being there for your children involves avoiding a very real temptation that parents, especially fathers, often face. It is the temptation of climbing the corporate ladder at the expense of time with your children. In such cases, parents try to basically buy their children's affections and love through getting them anything the child may want. And so often the parent gets upset when confronted about his (her) lack of time with the child and says something like, "The reason I'm working so many hours is to provide for my child the best that life has to offer." I would like to relate this to the passage we looked at previously from Exodus 33 of Moses and Israel entering the Promised Land. You may remember that even though Israel was so obstinate, God was still going to bring them into the Promised Land. Yet, His presence would not go with them, but He would send an angel before them. The people heard this sad word and went into mourning. Then Moses interceded by saying to God that if His presence didn't go with them, then don't lead them to the Promised Land. You see, the land flowing with milk and honey didn't mean anything if God's presence was not with them. The same is true today. Dad, you working so hard to provide material things for your children means little to them compared to your actual presence of being there for them. The best that life has to offer is not possessions, but your presence. Mike Singletary, the All-Pro and Hall of Fame linebacker for the Chicago Bears, stated, "...Fathers who are honest with themselves will admit that we all make mistakes. We have all made bad decisions. Some of those decisions have to be reversed. If you have accepted a promotion and a transfer that takes you up the corporate ladder at the expense of your kids, maybe you need to think about taking a step back. More important than providing a life of ease for your kids is making sure they know you love them unconditionally."[14] Even non-Christians know the necessity of this. Socrates once said, "Could I climb to the highest place in Athens, I would lift my voice and proclaim—Fellow citizens, why do ye turn and scrape every stone to gather wealth, and take so little care of your children, to whom one day you must relinquish it all?"[15] You see then, this is not a new problem, but has always been a challenge for parents. Being there for your children is much more important than anything material you could ever provide for them. I shared previously the story from G. Campbell Morgan about the daughter who took time away from her dad to make him slippers and he had told her that he would much rather have had the time with her that it took to make the slippers. Well, I'm sure that most children would say the same to their parents. They would much rather have our presence than all the time we spend seeking to provide material things for them.

At the same time, however, there is a sense in which providing for your children demonstrates that you are there for them. What do I mean? I mean providing, not for their material wants, but for their needs. Paul wrote in 1 Timothy 5:8, "But if anyone does not provide for his own, and especially for those of his household, he has denied the faith, and is worse than an unbeliever." And many times, for the parents to provide for their children's needs involves the parents making sacrifices, both in time and money. Here again, our heavenly Father is the perfect example for us to follow. In Matthew 6:8, Jesus teaches that our Father knows what we need even before we ask Him. Now, what was our greatest need? Salvation. And what did He do to meet that need? He made the tremendous sacrifice of sending His Son, the Lord Jesus Christ, to die on the cross to purchase our salvation and redeem us from Satan and sin.

I know there were many times that my parents made sacrifices to meet my needs, especially my medical needs. Someone once shared with me the story of a teenager who was taken to the doctor for an injury. The doctor recommended a certain wrap that cost less than $50. After the appointment the teenager asked the parent if they were going to get the wrap. The parent responded that they were not going to pay that price just for a wrap. And from what I was told, purchasing this wrap would not have been a sacrifice for this family. What did that possibly say to that teenager? I will provide for your needs as long as it isn't too expensive. Thus, that teenager could question as to whether or not the parents would really be there to meet further needs in the future. As parents meet their children's needs, even if it means a sacrifice, it shows their children that they are there for them.

A final practical way of making sure you are there for your children involves keeping the promises you have made to them. We know from Scripture that all promises from our heavenly Father are yes in Christ Jesus (2 Corinthians 1:20). How often do we as parents make promises to our children, especially promises that we will do something with them and then break them? When I think of this I'm reminded of Sandy and Harry Chapin's song, "Cat's in the Cradle." The lyrics of that song are extremely heartbreaking. They depict a life of unfulfilled promises from a dad to his son. The song speaks of a son being born to a family but the father had planes to catch and bills to pay, which prevented him from being there. His son learned to walk while the dad was away and before he knew it, the son was talking and as he grew he said, "I'm gonna be like you, dad. You know I'm gonna be like you." The son would ask his dad when he was coming home to which the dad always responded, "I don't know when, But we'll get together then. You know we'll have a good time then." When his son turned ten, his dad gave him a ball. The following dialogue occurred. The son said, "Thanks for the ball, dad, come on let's play. Can you teach me to throw?' I (dad) said, 'Not today, I got a lot to do.' He said, 'That's ok.' And he walked away, but his smile never dimmed, Said, 'I'm gonna be like him, yeah, You know I'm gonna be like him.'" Later in life when the dad finally had time for the son, the son didn't have time for the dad. When the son came home from college, the dad recognized that his son was a man and he wanted him to sit for a while. The son, however, stated that what he really wanted was his dad's car keys and he would see him later. Now, it was the dad who was asking the son when he was coming home to which the son replied, "I don't know when, But we'll get together then, dad. You know we'll have a good time then." When the dad had been retired for several years he called his son who had moved away, wanting to see him. The son said, "I'd love to dad, if I could find the time. You see, my new job's a hassle, and the kid's got the flu, But it's sure nice talking to you, dad. It's been sure nice talking to you." When the dad hung up the phone, he realized that his son had truly grown up to be just like him. The dad had promised to be there for his son, but never was and unfortunately, his son did the same thing to his dad.

Mike Singletary gives another good thought for fathers to consider. "A father has to be careful of his promises because a real man will follow through…The key is priorities. If you set a date with your child and something comes up at the office, you'd better see if you can postpone the office business. Otherwise, you're telling the child exactly where he fits in your life."[16] I have a friend who asked his young daughter if he had ever made a promise to her and not kept it. Living in Florida, the young daughter had never seen snow. So, she reminded her father of a promise he had previously made some time back to take her to see snow. He felt convicted that so much time had passed and he had not kept his promise. When the next opportunity arose, he took his daughter north so that she could see snow. What was the father doing? Demonstrating to his daughter that she was a priority and that keeping his promise of doing something with her was also a priority.

The best way to summarize this principle was depicted in a commercial by Sea World in Orlando, Florida. It kept showing some of the animals in the park. It then printed out the following question. "How long has it been since your child was this close to a dolphin (it pictures a child petting a dolphin) or a polar bear (it pictures a polar bear with its paws against a glass window and a child's hands touching the class on the other side as if touching the polar bear's paws) or to you (it pictures a child swinging around on her father's shoulders)?" Parents, just as the heavenly Father longs to be there for His children, we need to seek to be there for our children.

Chapter Five

Teaching Your Children through Discipline

> You have not yet resisted to the point of shedding blood in your striving against sin; and you have forgotten the exhortation which is addressed to you as sons, "MY SON, DO NOT REGARD LIGHTLY THE DISCIPLINE OF THE LORD, NOR FAINT WHEN YOU ARE REPROVED BY HIM; FOR THOSE WHOM THE LORD LOVES HE DISCIPLINES, AND HE SCOURGES EVERY SON WHOM HE RECEIVES."
> It is for discipline that you endure; God deals with you as sons; for what son is there whom his father does not discipline? But if you are without discipline, of which all have become partakers, then you are illegitimate children and not sons. Furthermore, we had earthly fathers to discipline us, and we respected them; shall we not much rather be subject to the Father of spirits, and live? For they disciplined us for a short time as seemed best to them, but He disciplines us for our good, that we may share His holiness. All discipline for the moment seems not to be joyful, but sorrowful; yet to those who have been trained by it, afterwards it yields the peaceful fruit of righteousness.
> —Hebrews 12:4-11

In this chapter and the next we are going to focus on the principle of parents teaching their children, but from two different aspects. We will examine "Teaching Our Children Through Discipline" and then "Teaching Our Children Through Instruction and Example." At first thought we may think that teaching through discipline is the negative aspect of teaching while teaching through instruction and example is the positive aspect of teaching. That is probably because discipline is often very painful. In reality, however, they both are positive because of the desired end result. We know that the Bible teaches us that one of the responsibilities of parents is to train their children which is a preparation for life. And parents must realize that both of these aspects of teaching are essential. If parents aren't committed to both, then their children will not be properly prepared for life and raising the next generation. The one aspect that especially seems to be missing today is discipline. As with all the other principles discussed in this book, our heavenly Father perfectly disciplines His children and parents need to learn from Him and thus, imitate Him as they teach their children through discipline.

One of the wrong concepts that some Christians have of God is that He is like a grandfather. What do grandparents often do to their grandchildren? They spoil them. God, our loving Father, did not adopt His children to spoil them. Rather, He adopted them to sanctify them, which is essential for as Hebrews 12:14 states, without sanctification no one will see the Lord. Consequently, part of that sanctifying process, which our Father is concerned about, includes teaching His children through discipline. Now, before we look at Hebrews 12:4-11 which speaks of that discipline, there are two important observations that we need to consider.

The first observation is to notice that I mentioned our Father's discipline for His children and not His punishment. Our Father does not punish His children. Why? Our punishment was taken care of at the cross by Jesus Christ when He died in our place and secured our pardon. Samuel Bolton wrote, "Sin is the cause of all punishment, punishment is the effect of sin. If God takes away the cause, namely sin, then too He takes away the effect, which is the punishment of sin. If the body is removed, the shadow goes too. Sin is the body and punishment the shadow; take away the sin and the punishment must needs be taken away. This seems to be implied in that phrase which is used in Scripture for the pardon of sin: 'I will remember your sins no more.' That is, never to condemn you for them, nor to charge them against you, nor yet to punish you for them. Where God pardons sin, there He forgives the punishment." So, the child of God never has to worry about being punished by God because we are positionally right or justified before God our Father through Christ's finished work at Calvary. Yet practically, we still have to deal with sin in our lives and the process of sanctification is the process whereby we sin less. In other words, we are released more and more from the power and pleasure of sin. How does our Father accomplish such? By disciplining His children. And we must never forget that this discipline comes from a loving Father. As Bolton wrote, "Discipline is our loving Father's medicine, not His punishment; His chastisement, not His sentence; His correction, not His condemnation."

A second observation that we need to emphasize relates to suffering. It is important that we remember that not all suffering is a result of sin. Yes, we may suffer as a result of sin and such would be part of the Father's discipline, but please don't think that if you are suffering, it is only a result of your sin. Job suffered extensively from Satan and it was because he was righteous. Both Testaments record saints who suffered extensively because of their faith. And of course, Jesus suffered to the utmost and He had no sin. Consequently, even though we may suffer at the hands of wicked men or Satan's demonic forces, such suffering is filtered through our sovereign Father's fingers of love. He then takes that suffering at the hands of the wicked and uses it as a means of training us and conforming us to the image of Jesus. Leon Morris wrote, "The writer points to the importance of discipline and proceeds to show that for Christians suffering is rightly understood only when seen as God's Fatherly discipline, correcting and directing us. Suffering is evidence, not that God does not love us, but that He does."[1] With these two observations in mind, we now want to examine our Father teaching His children through discipline in Hebrews 12:4-11 by looking at four truths.

The first truth, in verse 4, emphasizes the position that the recipients of this letter were then in. The author writes, "You have not yet resisted to the point of shedding blood in your striving against sin." The picture here is related to sports but the author has changed it from a race (Hebrews 12:1) to boxing which often involves the shedding of blood from vicious blows to the head.[2] Simon Kistemaker wrote, "The imagery of withstanding the opponent to the point of shedding blood serves as a parallel to the reader's struggle against sin. No specific sin is mentioned. Sin, however, with its mysterious power is a formidable opponent that must be resisted unto death."[3] Even though a specific sin is not mentioned, in light of the context of Hebrews 10:32-11:40, it could refer to the sin of unbelief. So, the author is encouraging them to resist sin, especially the sin of unbelief, even if it means persecution and martyrdom. As R.C.H. Lenski wrote, "This sin would win if in fear of blood the readers would relinquish their faith; it would be vanquished if the readers, unafraid of a bloody death, held fast to their faith."[4] Hebrews 10:32-34 records the great conflict of sufferings they had endured. They had been "made a public spectacle through reproaches and tribulations." They had "accepted joyfully the seizure of (their) property." Now, however, their position was more a period of rest, which could cause spiritual laxness. Consequently, they must never forget what Jesus endured (verses 2-3) and that they may face the same. So, their position now was not nearly as difficult as others whom the author had previously mentioned. Even if they should suffer, however, it is part of a loving Father's discipline.

The second truth from this passage, verse 5, focuses on what our perception is to be toward the Father's discipline. In other words, how are we to view or comprehend His discipline? In order to understand this fully, here again, we must focus on the context.

Hebrews 11:35-38 lists some of the tremendous afflictions that many of the Old Testament saints had experienced as a result of their faith. They were tortured, experienced mockings and scourgings, even chains and imprisonment. They were stoned, sawn in two, tempted, put to death with the sword, and even went about in sheepskins, goatskins, being destitute, afflicted, ill-treated, wandering in deserts, mountains, caves and holes in the ground. Hebrews 12:1 emphasizes that we are to lay aside the sin which so easily entangles us in order to run with endurance the race that is set before us, but we are also to lay aside every encumbrance. How do we do that? Hebrews 12:2 tells us that we are to fix our eyes on Jesus, the author and perfecter of faith. And let's recall what Jesus had to go through before He sat down at the right hand of the Father. He had to endure the cross, despise the shame and endure hostility by sinners (verses 2-3). In other words, He had to endure afflictions, trials and persecutions even though He was the perfect Son of God who had no sin. Yet, as we've seen previously from Hebrews 5:8, He learned obedience from the things which He suffered. Alistair Begg wrote, "it was in the experiences of affliction and rejection and difficulty that Jesus' obedience became full-grown. If, then, suffering was the means by which Jesus, who was sinless, became mature, how much more do we need it in our sinfulness!"[5]

So, what is the context of this Scripture pointing to? Our heavenly Father uses afflictions, trials, and persecutions as a means to discipline His children and sanctify them. Some of these come directly from His hand and others are permitted by Him, but the bottom line is to realize that He sovereignly ordains and uses them all to discipline us.

When you think of discipline, what do you usually think of? Probably most of us relate it to a spanking or grounding or time out or something similar. In other words, we think of it in a negative connotation as a means of correcting a certain behavior that is inappropriate. The Greek word for discipline certainly includes this, but it also involves much more. It actually refers to the whole training and education of children. It speaks of the cultivation of the mind and morals. So, it involves both correction and instruction. You see, in Judaism the father was required to provide for the instruction of his children and to teach them good behavior. Thus, there was instruction and appropriate corrective measures. The same is true with our heavenly Father.

Obviously, the recipients of this letter were having problems with some of the afflictions they were experiencing and what their purpose was. Consequently, the writer of Hebrews points to the fact they had forgotten what God's word says and reminds them of Proverbs 3:11-12. In other words, what you are going through is not something new, but it is a principle from the Old Testament. And this principle points to receiving with meekness discipline from our heavenly Father. Hebrews 12:5 is taken from Proverbs 3:11.

In this verse we see two perceptions we are to have concerning the Father's discipline. First, we are not to regard it lightly. The words "regard lightly" mean to make light of something, to care little for or to neglect. It speaks then of treating something as insignificant. So, what does this mean? When we are facing afflictions, trials or persecutions, don't neglect or treat as insignificant what our Father is trying to teach us through them. He, in His sovereignty, is using these things to discipline or train us. Well, how can we regard lightly His discipline? We can do it by complaining. Such an attitude says to God that He doesn't know what He is doing. A prime example of this is Israel in its wilderness journey. Deuteronomy 8:2-6 states: "And you shall remember all the way which the LORD your God has led you in the wilderness these forty years, that He might humble you, testing you, to know what was in your heart, whether you would keep His commandments or not. And He humbled you and let you be hungry, and fed you with manna which you did not know, nor did your fathers know, that He might make you understand that man does not live by bread alone, but man lives by everything that proceeds out of the mouth of the LORD. Your clothing did not wear out on you, nor did your foot swell these forty years. Thus you are to know in your heart that the LORD your God was disciplining you just as a man disciplines his son. Therefore, you shall keep the commandments of the LORD your God, to walk in His ways and fear Him." Did you notice why God tested them and let them be hungry and fed them with manna? He was disciplining them as a man disciplines his son. He wanted them to learn the fear of the LORD. Yet, we know that Israel really regarded lightly His discipline. How do we know that? Through their constant complaining and disobedience, which demonstrated that they didn't learn the fear of the LORD. Numbers 14:22 states that Israel tested God ten times and did not listen to His voice. They were basically saying that God didn't know what He was doing. Psalm 119:75b, however, states: "And that in faithfulness Thou hast afflicted me." So, whatever affliction (discipline) God has brought about or is allowing us to experience stems from His faithfulness, which means that He can't make a mistake. That is why we read of Paul's admonitions in Philippians 2:12-15: "So then, my beloved, just as you have always obeyed, not as in my presence only, but now much more in my absence, work out your salvation with fear and trembling; for it is God who is at work in you, both to will and to work for His good pleasure. Do all things without grumbling or disputing; that you may prove yourselves to be blameless and innocent, children of God above reproach in the midst of a crooked and perverse generation, among whom you appear as lights in the world."

You see, in the midst of our afflictions (discipline), God is at work in us for His good pleasure. Therefore, if we see them all as coming from God our Father, then we can better accept them and don't need to complain about them. Please understand, this does not mean that in the midst of afflictions that we can't be honest with our Father and tell Him that we are hurting. It doesn't mean that we can't pray that He would bring us out of the affliction. There are numerous Scriptures in the Bible, especially the Psalms, that are requests and prayers that God would deliver them from the afflictions they were facing. Judges 2:18 speaks of God being moved with pity at Israel's groaning because of those who oppressed and afflicted them. Psalm 9:12b says: "He does not forget the cry of the afflicted." Psalm 72 is a Psalm of Solomon that describes the reign of a righteous king. Verse 12 states: "For he will deliver the needy when he cries for help, The afflicted also, and him who has no helper." Now, if a righteous, though imperfect, earthly king will deliver the needy, then how much more will the sovereign King of the universe, Who is perfectly righteous, do even more so. You see, there is a big difference between crying out to God when we are hurting versus complaining about God and what He has ordained for us to go through as a means of disciplining us whereby we will learn the fear of the LORD.

This is further clarified in a second way that we can regard lightly His discipline and that is to question Him or doubt Him. James 1 speaks of experiencing trials and in the midst of them we can ask God for wisdom, but we must ask in faith. So, it is not wrong to question God in the midst of discipline to ask Him what He is trying to teach us, but we must ask in faith. We regard lightly His discipline, however, when we question Him in the sense of trying to challenge Him. For example, when a parent tells a child to do something and the child asks "Why?" what is the child doing? Most of the time the child isn't looking for the real reason why, but is challenging the parent to justify their actions. We do the same to our heavenly Father if we question Him without faith. Therefore, our first perception toward the Father's discipline is that we are not to regard it lightly.

The second perception toward the Father's discipline is that we are not to faint when we are reproved by Him. The word "faint" is the same word as "lose heart" in verse 3. It means to have one's strength relaxed or to be enfeebled or to become faint-hearted. It basically points to becoming despondent, depressed, or hopeless. And the word "reproved" means to convict, to expose, to bring to light, or to find fault with. Consequently, this points to the fact that God uses afflictions, trials or persecutions as a means of His discipline to expose or bring to light areas in our lives that need correcting. In other words, we are not to become hopeless or depressed in the midst of these afflictions. Many times, though, we become spiritually inept and unresponsive to what our Father is trying to do in our lives. How often do we feel like the Psalmist in Psalm 42:11ab: "Why are you in despair, O my soul? And why have you become disturbed within me?" What is the solution? Psalm 42:11cd gives the answer. "Hope in God, for I shall yet praise Him, The help of my countenance, and my God." So, our second perception or view toward the Father's discipline is that we don't need to be faint-hearted or hopeless.

What then does verse 5 really point to? It really points to the fact that in the midst of afflictions, trials or persecutions, our primary focus is not to be on the experience of them, but rather we are to focus on our Father and what He wants to do for us and in us through the disciplining experience. Summarizing the two perceptions of verse 5, Geoffrey Wilson wrote, "Although the hard-hearted man steels himself against feeling the stroke, and the faint-hearted man reels under it, the child of God is neither to despise correction nor to despair when he is reproved; otherwise he will fail to profit from the experience."[6]

The third truth from this passage, verses 6-8, deals with the proofs in discipline. The Father's discipline proves two things. First, it proves that He loves us as we see in verse 6a. This verse comes from Proverbs 3:12a, but Proverbs 3:12b says: "Even as a father, the son in whom he delights." The word "delights" speaks of acceptance and means to be well-pleased. Do you see what this means? Our Father delights or is well-pleased with His children. And whenever He disciplines us, it is in perfect love. Parent, when you were growing up, did your parents ever tell you before spanking you, "This is going to hurt me more than it does you." Of course, you didn't believe them until you became a parent yourself and spanked one of your own children. Why is that true? Because it comes from a loving parent. Do you realize that is the same with our heavenly Father? Our Father's discipline of His children stems from His love. As Lamentations 3:31-33 states: "For the Lord will not reject forever, For if He causes grief, Then He will have compassion According to His abundant lovingkindness. For He does not afflict willingly, Or grieve the sons of men." Consequently, when our Father disciplines His children, it is always tempered with His mercy. As Psalms 89:30-33 states: "If his sons forsake My law, And do not walk in My judgments, If they violate My statutes, And do not keep My commandments, Then I will visit their transgression with the rod, And their iniquity with stripes. But I will not break off My lovingkindness from him, Nor deal falsely in My faithfulness." Thomas Lye wrote, "When our heavenly Father is, as it were, forced to put forth His anger, He then makes use of a father's rod, not an executioner's axe. He will neither break His children's bones, nor His own covenant. He lashes in love, in measure, in pity, and compassion."[7]

Second, the Father's discipline proves that we are truly His children as recorded in verses 6b-8. Two observations to make from these verses. First, notice that His discipline is a sign that He has accepted us (verse 6b). The word "receives" means to admit or to accept. Every person that comes to God through repentance of sin and faith in Jesus Christ as personal Lord and Savior is received as a child of God. John 1:12 says: "But as many as received Him, to them He gave the right to become children of God, even to those who believe in His name." Thus, as a child of God, our Father, at times scourges us and this literally means to beat with a whip. To put it in modern terms, our Father spanks us, His children, out of love. At this point we need to understand a very important truth. It expands upon what I wrote earlier about suffering being a result of sin. Sadly, there are those who teach that if you are suffering in any way, it demonstrates the sin of a lack of faith. In reality, they are saying that God is displeased with your lack of faith and that is why you are suffering. Robert Traill wrote, though, "It is a common, but sinful way of arguing with many Christians, that they are not God's children, because they are so much corrected by Him. To question our state because of affliction, or to conclude our state to be good because of prosperity and ease, are equally false and foolish, though not equally dangerous; for it is far more so, falsely to conclude a good state when it is not, than unbelieving to disturb a good state where it is."[8] Please realize, Robert Traill died in 1716. Can you imagine what he would say about some of the prosperity preachers on television if he lived today? John Colquhoun wrote, "When waters of a full cup are measured out to you, do not conclude that God does not love you, or that you are not one of His children. For great as your distresses are, they are not only consistent with His love for you, but they proceed from it."[9] You see then, as one Puritan stated, God's love and God's rod may stand together. Why does He do this to His children?

This points to the second observation and that is He spanks or disciplines us because He takes seriously His responsibility as a parent (Verses 7-8). Philip Hughes wrote, "Discipline is the mark not of a harsh and heartless father but of a father who is deeply and lovingly concerned for the well-being of his son."[10] You see, divine discipline points to divine love, which points to divine responsibility. So, as children endure discipline from their earthly fathers, we are to do the same from our heavenly Father. And the word "endure" means to patiently endure the discipline. It refers to a spirit that bears things, not just with resignation, but with hope knowing that this discipline is leading to a goal of glory. As 2 Corinthians 4:17 says, "For momentary, light affliction is producing for us an eternal weight of glory far beyond all comparison."

Therefore, in verse 7 the author compares God disciplining His children to that of an earthly father. We will deal with this more when we make application of it for parents, but the importance of this is found in verse 8. No discipline by our Father shows that a person is an illegitimate child and not a son. In other words, such a person has God as his Father in the sense that He created him, but not as a loving Father through adoption as sons whereby he can call Him, "Abba, Father." There are two important truths that we need to consider. First, whereas God may extend grace even to those who are not His children, He only disciplines His true children. Alistair Begg gives a beautiful example of this in his book, *Made for His Pleasure*. His family has a trampoline and he states that when he comes home in the evening there may be several children playing on it. He can offer each of those children a cold drink to refresh themselves. If, however, all of the children are breaking the rules of safety while playing on it, he can only legitimately discipline the three which are his children. He writes, "The cold drink may be shared by all and any, the discipline experienced by a few."[11] Consequently, as Henry Smith wrote, "An obedient child doth not only kiss the hand which giveth, but the rod which beateth."[12] You see, the Bible states that God allows the sun to shine on the righteous and the unrighteous. He gives rain to both. Such gifts to the unrighteous come from God's common grace. Yes, they may be recipients of His common grace, but they are not recipients of His Fatherly love because they are without discipline and are as illegitimate sons.

Have you ever been in a mall and seen a child really acting awfully and think to yourself, *I would love to have that child for a week*? But what happens? You soon forget about that child because you don't love that child as your own and don't feel the responsibility for that child. Why? He or she isn't your child. In our society, a father usually feels very little love and responsibility for an illegitimate child. Isn't that the reason we hear of paternity suits, trying to get a father to take responsibility for an illegitimate child? Lewis Bayly wrote, "Yea, it is a sure note, that where God seeth sin and smites not, there He detests and loves not; therefore it is said, that He suffered the wicked sons of Eli to continue their sins, without correction, 'Because the Lord would slay them.' On the other side, there is no surer token of God's Fatherly love and care, than to be corrected with some cross, as oft as we commit any sinful crime. Affliction, therefore, is a seal of adoption, no sign of reprobation; for the purest corn is cleanest fanned, the finest gold is oftest tried, the sweetest grape is hardest pressed, and the truest Christian heaviest crossed."[13]

The second truth to consider is a contrast between God's dealings with His children versus those who aren't. This goes back to something mentioned previously. Whereas God disciplines His children, He punishes His enemies. Discipline is a sign of parental love while punishment is a sign of judicial wrath. John Howe wrote, "When once He is reconciled to you, He no longer treats you as enemies; if sometimes He sees a cause to afflict His own, He smites them not as He smites those that smote them." And Charles Bridge wrote, "The same hand-but not the same character-gives the stroke, to the godly and the ungodly. The scourge of the Judge is widely different from the rod of the Father."[14] When we are disciplined by our heavenly Father, we should be thankful because it proves He loves us and that we are truly His children. In other words, we need to claim the words of Job 5:17a, "Behold, how happy is the man whom God reproves."

The final truth from this passage, verses 9-11, concerning the Father's discipline focuses on the purposes for His discipline. Three purposes are mentioned. The first purpose of His discipline is life. In verse 9 we see that we had earthly fathers who disciplined us and we respected them. Of course, we are disciplined by our earthly fathers until we reach maturity. As a child of God, however, we are always under the discipline (training) of our heavenly Father. If we respect or reverence our earthly fathers for their discipline, how much more should we be subject to the Father of our spirits and live? The word "subject" means to put in subjection, to submit one's control or to yield or obey one's admonition or advice. And why should we do this? In order to live. There are two aspects we need to view this from. First, failure to submit to our Father's discipline may end in physical death. Deuteronomy 21:18-21 records a man with a stubborn and rebellious son who disobeyed both parents and when they chastised him, he would not listen to them. So, they took their son to the elders of the city and informed them of his disobedience and refusal to obey. This resulted in the son being stoned to death by the men of the city. Why was the son put to death? Because he was rebellious and refused to submit to their discipline. We have some New Testament Scriptures which point to the same thing from our heavenly Father. In 1 Corinthians 11 Paul warns the Corinthian Christians of partaking of the Lord's Supper in an unworthy manner. What happened to some who did take it in a wrong way? First Corinthians 11:30 states, "For this reason many among you are weak and sick, and a number sleep." And when Paul mentions those who sleep, he is referring to those who died as a means of discipline. Our first thought may be, "that is so drastic," but even this comes from a loving Father and it proves that a person is truly His child, for 1 Corinthians 11:32 says, "But when we are judged, we are disciplined by the Lord in order that we may not be condemned along with the world." If there was no discipline, then such a person is not a true child of God and thus, is condemned with the rest of the world. But, there is a second aspect to being subject to the Father of spirits and living. When a child of God does submit and patiently endures His discipline, he will have a fuller, more abundant life. Why?

This leads to the second purpose of His discipline and that is, that we may share His holiness, found in verse 10. We see that the earthly father's discipline is for a short time as seemed best to them. What does this mean? Two things. First, as stated previously, a parent's discipline is really for the short period until the child reaches maturity and is independent of the parent. Second, it means that earthly parents are not infallible. They can make mistakes in their discipline.

We never have to worry about our heavenly Father making mistakes in His discipline. This verse tells us that He disciplines us for our good, for our benefit or for our advantage. Let's contrast this then with what we saw of an earthly father's discipline in the previous paragraph. Rather than the discipline being for a short time until we are independent of our earthly parents, our heavenly Father's discipline is for our entire life whereby we will constantly be dependent upon Him. And then, our heavenly Father knows the right discipline to bring about His intended purpose—that we may share His holiness. As John Calvin wrote, "Mortal men chastise their children as they think good, but God applies His discipline with the wisest purpose and the highest wisdom so that there is nothing in it that is out of control."[15] That fits in with what Paul wrote in Romans 8:28-29b: "And we know that God causes all things to work together for good to those who love God, to those who are called according to His purpose. For whom He foreknew, He also predestined to become conformed to the image of His Son." Thus, our loving heavenly Father will use all afflictions, trials, and persecutions as a part of His perfect discipline and cause them to work together for our good which is our being conformed to the image of His Son which is being separated more and more from sin which is sharing His holiness. Summarizing this contrast between our earthly fathers and our heavenly Father, A.B. Davidson wrote, "It is not the duration of the chastisement that is the point of the passage; it is the duration of our relation in each case to him who chastens."[16] That is why we aren't to regard lightly His discipline or faint or lose heart in whatever we face. Our Father is using that to correct us and instruct us to make us more like Jesus.

But there is a third purpose for His discipline and that is it yields the peaceful fruit of righteousness, as found in verse 11. We read that discipline is not pleasant or joyful, but sorrowful. In other words, while you're being disciplined, it is not much fun. Think about it, though. If discipline wasn't painful, would there be any correction or profit come from it? Not at all. That is why this verse mentions being trained by it. The word "trained" means to exercise and we get our English word "gymnastics" from it. So, this word pictures the disciplined life of one who works out in the gym. If you've ever been around athletes as they exercise or train, you probably have heard the expression, "No pain, no gain." Thus, if you want the desired result, you must be willing to experience pain. The same is true here. Our heavenly Father has ordained for us to go through painful afflictions, trials, and persecutions as a means of disciplining us, but notice what it produces. The peaceful fruit of righteousness. Writing of the adjective "peaceful," J.B. Moffatt wrote, "The writer might be throwing out a hint to his readers, that suffering was apt to render people irritable, impatient with one another's faults. The later record even of the martyrs, for example, shows that the very prospect of death did not always prevent Christians from quarreling in prison."[17] So, this verse speaks of continually being trained whereby the peaceful fruit of righteousness is displayed. As Leon Morris wrote, "It is important that suffering be accepted in the right spirit; otherwise it does not produce the right result. It is not a matter of accepting a minor chastisement or two with good grace; it is the habit of life that is meant."[18] It is important to realize that through discipline our Father is seeking to build in our character love, faith, and righteousness which is walking by the Spirit and displaying the fruit of the Spirit as Galatians 5 tells us.

What then do all these purposes relate to? All three purposes of discipline point to the fact that we will be drawn closer in our relationship to our loving heavenly Father. Consequently, if our heavenly Father did not discipline His children, it would be unloving. As John Trapp wrote, "Corrections are pledges of our adoption and badges of our sonship. One Son God hath without sin, but none without sorrow. As God corrects none but His own, so all that are His shall be sure to have it, and they take it for a favour too."[19] At this point we need to ask ourselves a question. How do we react to the afflictions, trials, sufferings, and persecutions that our loving Father sends for us to experience in order to discipline us? Do we regard them lightly, or lose heart or faint or lose hope? If so, please realize that our Father is disciplining us not to destroy us, but to develop and conform us to make us like Jesus. Parents are to view discipline in a similar way in that they are not trying to destroy their children but to develop and prepare them for a life that will glorify God. That is why it is so important that parents not discipline out of anger, but love.

This principle of teaching our children through discipline is so important for our society today because it is so neglected. That is why I believe teenage drug addiction, teenage pregnancy, and teenage crime are so high. Now I personally believe that even if a non-Christian is obedient to God's principles, as found in His Word, he will be blessed to a degree. Truly, he won't be obeying from the proper motives and he may not even know that he is obeying Scripture, but God's common grace may bless him. This is especially true when it comes to discipline. The Minnesota Crime Commission included the following in a report they issued:

"Every baby starts life as a little savage. He is completely selfish and self-centered. He wants what he wants when he wants it; his bottle, his mother's attention, his playmate's toys, his uncle's watch, or whatever. Deny him these and he seethes with rage and aggressiveness, which would be murderous were he not so helpless. He's dirty, he has no morals, no knowledge, no developed skills. This means that all children, not just certain children but all children, are born delinquent. If permitted to continue in their self-centered world of infancy, given free reign to their impulsive actions to satisfy each want, every child would grow up to be a criminal, a thief, a killer, a rapist."[20]

What does that report point to? The Biblical doctrine of the total depravity of man. As Gardiner Spring wrote, "The history of man in all ages shows that good is not natural to the human heart; individual consciousness shows it. The mind is not even indifferent to good and evil; its predilections are in favor of evil. No child needs to be taught, persuaded, or coerced to what is wrong."[21] That is why we are examining the principle of teaching through discipline before we examine teaching through instruction and example. Parents can teach their children through discipline much earlier than they can teach them through instruction and example.

There are several truths to be considered regarding parents teaching their children through discipline. And our focus will be on the corrective part of discipline. The first truth is that both parents are to be involved in discipline. Hebrews 12:9 only mentions fathers and in Ephesians 6:4, only fathers are mentioned to bring up their children in the discipline of the Lord, but so many other Scriptures point to the truth that both parents are to be involved in the raising of children to include discipline, instruction, and example.

The second truth is to understand the reasons for parents disciplining their children. Several reasons are given in the book of Proverbs. First, discipline is a means of removing moral insolence. Proverbs 22:15 states, "Foolishness is bound up in the heart of a child; The rod of discipline will remove it far from him." Don Kistler, President of Soli Deo Gloria Ministries wrote, "According to that verse, moral insolence is tied with a rope to the heart of a child, for that is what the words mean. It is not simply the idea of silliness or childishness, it is the idea of moral insolence, a moral weakness that manifests itself in silliness or childishness. There is to be sure, a silliness in children, for, after all, they are just that, children. But the sinful ways in which that is manifested are not to be tolerated, but are to be disciplined out of them! That is what 'the rod of discipline' is to do!"[22]

Many verses in Proverbs speak of the rod of discipline. What does that point to? A physical result to a child's disobedience. When I was a little boy I use to get, as a gift, a "bolo paddle." It was a paddle that had a rubber band attached to it with a small ball at the end of the rubber band. Of course, the rubber band would quickly break and my parents then used the paddle as a very effective "rod of discipline." In fact, after my brother and I grew up, my mother painted one of the paddles and wrote on it, "Recipe for Good Boys" and hung it as a decoration in her kitchen. We often hear the saying, "spare the rod and spoil the child." There is so much truth to that and this will be shown further in the next reason for discipline.

A second reason for discipline is that it is a means of protection for our children. Proverbs 19:18 states, "Discipline your son while there is hope, And do not desire his death." And Proverbs 23:13-14 says, "Do not hold back discipline from the child, Although you beat him with the rod, he will not die. You shall beat him with the rod, And deliver his soul from Sheol." There are two aspects from which we need to view this as it relates to death. The first aspect deals with a premature physical death. Why do so many teenagers commit suicide, become involved in drugs and gangs and other crimes, which end in death? Two quotes by J. Edgar Hoover, the former director of the FBI, are very appropriate to consider. He stated, "Criminals are home-grown," and "The cure for crime is not the electric chair but the high chair."[23] A mother once asked a psychologist, "When shall I start training my child?" The psychologist asked, "How old is he?" to which the mother responded, "Five." The psychologist then said, "Madam, hurry home! You have already lost five years."[24] Remember what Proverbs 19:18a stated, "Discipline your son while there is hope." That hope is when they are young because if parents wait, there will come a time when it is too late to discipline. Do you know this is proven in Scripture? In 1 Samuel 3, Samuel receives his prophetic call from God. In verse 13 God tells Samuel concerning Eli, "For I have told him that I am about to judge his house forever for the iniquity which he knew, because his sons brought a curse on themselves and he did not rebuke them." What was the nature of Eli's lack of discipline? First Samuel 2:22-24 tells us. "Now Eli was very old; and he heard all that his sons were doing to Israel, and how they lay with the women who served at the doorway of the tent of meeting. And he said to them, 'Why do you do such thing, the evil things that I hear from all these people? No, my sons; for the report is not good which I hear the LORD'S people circulating." Did you notice the extent of his discipline? "No, my sons; for the report is not good which I hear." Obviously, he was not very active in his discipline of them. When I was growing up, my parents would always tell my school teachers and Sunday School teachers that if I didn't behave properly, they wanted to know and they would take the appropriate action to make sure my behavior improved. My parents took an active role in disciplining me. Because Eli didn't discipline his sons properly, both he and his sons died on the same day.

Another example of this is David and his son, Adonijah. Solomon was to be king, but Adonijah exalted himself and said, "I will be King." Why did he act in such a way? As 1 Kings 1:6 tells us, "And his father had never crossed him at any time by asking, 'Why have you done so?'" It seems that David was afraid to discipline his son because it might lead to Adonijah's displeasure. And I believe such a lack of discipline led to Adonijah's behavior which resulted in his execution as recorded in 1 Kings 3. Sadly, David's actions here are very similar with his actions toward Absalom, which led to Absalom's death. In other words, David neglected to properly discipline Adonijah and Absalom and they both died premature deaths.

There is a second aspect, however, in which we need to view discipline as a means of protection for our children as it relates to death. If there is no discipline, then parents are preparing their children to experience eternal death, which is separation from God's glorious presence. Kistler wrote, "he will perish if you don't correct him, and you would have to be the cruelest parents in the world if you didn't do what you could to keep your children from perishing! He will go to hell if you let him do what he wants. He may not go to hell if you correct him with discipline."[25]

A third reason for discipline is that it proves your love for your children. We've already seen that our heavenly Father disciplines His children because He loves them. Well, the same is to be true of earthly parents. Proverbs 13:24 states, "He who spares his rod hates his son, But he who loves him disciplines him diligently." The last part of that verse literally means, "But he who loves him seeks him diligently with discipline." There are two ways that we demonstrate love for our children through discipline. First, our discipline will teach them the fear of the Lord. We've already seen from Deuteronomy 8 that God disciplined Israel so that they would learn to fear Him. When parents discipline their children they are teaching them to fear the Lord by fearing the parents. Kistler wrote, "The way children learn about sin is by the offenses they commit against their parents, so it would stand to reason that the way they learn about fearing God is to fear their parents."[26]

A second way that parents demonstrate love for their children is that through discipline they show a concern for their children's salvation. Arthur Hildersham was an English Puritan preacher of the 17th century. He wrote over 700 pages in a commentary on Psalm 51:1-7. Several sermons were from verse 5 in which he dealt with the inherent sin that is in children. He saw discipline as one of two means that God has established to drive out the natural corruption in children. He wrote, "Physical consequences to disobedience are a special means commended to us by the Holy Ghost in Scripture, and sanctified to the end that we might abate the strength of natural corruption in children, and to make them capable of saving. And therefore it is to be observed in the law that no child was reputed to be graceless or past hope until he had showed himself not only unteachable, but incorrigible also, until his parents had used means to reform him not only by counsel, instruction and reproof, but by correcting, and chastisement also, and all in vain."[27]

John and Charles Wesley's mother, Susannah, raised 17 children. She stated about raising children: "The parent who studies to subdue self-will in his child works together with God in the renewing and saving of a soul. The parent who indulges it does the devil's work, makes religion impracticable, salvation unattainable, and does all that in him lies to damn his child, body and soul, forever."[28] There is no greater love that a parent should have for his children than that his children have a saving relationship with God the Father through the Lord Jesus Christ. Thus, it is essential that parents discipline their children.

A fourth reason why parents are to discipline their children is that it honors God and His word. We know that the fifth commandment is, "Honor your father and your mother" (Exodus 20:12a). Paul mentions that also in Ephesians 6 in the context of children obeying their parents in the Lord for this is right (verse 1). Thus, when parents discipline their children, they are teaching them to honor their parents which honors the Lord. Not to discipline them, however, honors the children, which in turn dishonors the Lord. It would be as if parents had rather displease the Lord than their children.[29] We've already seen examples of that with David and Eli from Scripture.

A final reason why parents are to discipline their children is the comfort and blessing and delight it will bring the parents. Proverbs 29:17 states, "Correct your son, and he will give you comfort; He will also delight your soul." The converse of that, however, is found in Proverbs 29:15, "The rod and reproof give wisdom, But a child who gets his own way brings shame to his mother." In the

August 1960 issue of the Ladies Home Journal, there was an article entitled, "I Reared a Criminal." It told the heartbreaking story from the mother's perspective of her and her husband's failure to discipline their son. She stated: "we loved him, but his father was too busy to be with him when he was young. I couldn't bring myself to punish him for misbehavior. We sided against his teachers when they complained about his work (and conduct) in school. As he grew up he would hardly discuss the time of day with us. He was expelled from school. We gave him money so he wouldn't steal again. I wept when the police called and I had to turn my boy over to them...As I watched them search him my life seemed to end."[30] Did you notice the regret in that mother's story? I'm sure that if she could start over, she would have raised her son differently to include the "rod of discipline." This is a perfect example of what we saw previously from Proverbs 19:18 of disciplining our children while there is hope. As Thomas Guthrie wrote, "If a parent does not punish his sons, his sons will be sure to punish him."[31]

Parents, as stated before, children are a precious gift to us from the Lord. And when we are given such a gift we are to treat them in a responsible way. Not to discipline our children is irresponsible and unfortunately, demonstrates to them that we really don't love them and don't care about their salvation or their future. Aren't you thankful that we, as Christians, have a loving Father who loves us enough to discipline us for His glory and our good? Let's seek to imitate Him in teaching our children through disciplining them. It is for their good.

Chapter Six

Teaching Your Children through Instruction and Example

All Scripture is inspired by God and profitable
for teaching, for reproof, for correction, for
training in righteousness; that the man of
God may be adequate, equipped
for every good work.
—2 Timothy 3:16-17

"Hear, O Israel! The LORD is our God,
the LORD is one! And you shall love the
LORD your God with all your heart and
with all your soul and with all your might.
And these words, which I am commanding
you today, shall be on your heart; and you
shall teach them diligently to your sons and
shall talk of them when you sit in your
house and when you walk by the way
and when you lie down and when you
rise up. And you shall bind them as a
sign on your hand and they shall be as
frontals on your forehead. And you
shall write them on the doorposts
of your house and on your gates."
—Deuteronomy 6:4-9

We now come to the principle of teaching our children through instruction and example. As was depicted in the last chapter and now in this chapter, there are several different ways for teaching to occur. In fact, the definition of teaching as recorded in most dictionaries would include the words instruction and example and the word "discipline" is a synonym for teaching. What then is the purpose of all these words as it relates to teaching? It is to impart knowledge and skill.[1] Instruction would speak of a methodical direction in a certain subject.[2] Example would relate to modeling or imitating a particular action. Discipline refers to training in behavior and the exercise of self-control.[3] You could say then, that a person's entire life includes some type of teaching whether it involves academics, athletics, occupations, or even hobbies just to mention a few. Unfortunately, the most important aspect of teaching that is so often neglected is how to live a life that glorifies God. Question 1 of the Shorter Catechism of the *Westminster Confession of Faith* asks, "What is the chief end of man?" The answer is, "Man's chief end is to glorify God, and to enjoy Him forever." In other words, how to live in relationship with God our Father and enjoy that relationship for all eternity. That was the purpose for which we were created.

When God created Adam and placed him in the Garden of Eden, even before He created Eve as a helper suitable for Adam, God instructed Adam. His instruction was that Adam could eat freely from any tree in the garden except for the tree of the knowledge of good and evil, for in the day he would eat of that tree he would surely die. What was the nature of God's instruction? How Adam could continue to live in a way that glorified God and enjoy the intimate relationship into which he was created for as Ecclesiastes 7:29 states, God made man upright. As we all too well know, Adam and Eve didn't obey God's instruction and thus, sin entered the world which resulted in man becoming dead in his trespasses and sins (Ephesians 2:1). In other words, because of sin there was a separation between God and man (Isaiah 59:2) and man could do nothing to restore the relationship he had been created into with God.

After Adam and Eve ate the forbidden fruit, they recognized their sin(their nakedness) and upon hearing the sound of the LORD God walking in the garden, they hid themselves. Genesis 3 records God, in His grace, seeking them out and confronting them about their disobedience and Adam blames the woman whom God had given him and Eve blames the serpent. Then God speaks of the curses that would result due to their disobedience. Before God tells Adam and Eve of the curses that they and their posterity would experience, He curses the serpent (the devil). And in God's curse of the serpent, He gives the gospel of grace in embryo form in Genesis 3:15 when He states, "And I will put enmity Between you and the woman, And between your seed, and her seed; He shall bruise you on the head, And you shall bruise Him on the heel." Do you see what God is doing then? Not only is He cursing the serpent, but more importantly, He is instructing Adam and Eve about what He will do whereby mankind could be restored in his relationship with God. Remember Adam's condition prior to sin. He was able not to sin and thus, everything he did glorified God and he enjoyed an intimate relationship with God. In other words, he was able to fulfill the chief end for which he had been created as stated previously from the Westminster Confession. After his sin, however, it was totally impossible for him to fulfill it. Through the gospel message, taught by God, he could be restored in his relationship with God and seek to fulfill his chief end again.

We know that Adam and Eve believed the gospel message in Genesis 3:15 for in Genesis 3:21 we read that God made for them garments of skin to clothe them and cover their nakedness (their sin). Previously, after they had sinned and recognized their nakedness, they tried to cover it themselves by sewing fig leaves together in order to make for themselves loin coverings. Such was unacceptable to God, however, and that is why He made garments of skin for them to cover their sin. So, God shed the blood of an innocent animal to cover their sin. And they believed the message as demonstrated by their receiving these garments from God. This is a beautiful picture and shadow of what God did for us through

His Son, the Lord Jesus Christ, at the cross of Calvary. Christ died and shed His blood whereby we could be forgiven and clothed in His righteousness. When we trust in His finished work alone at Calvary on our behalf, we are clothed in His righteousness and thus, are restored in our relationship with God. Consequently, we are now able to live in such a way whereby we can fulfill the chief end for which we were created. How then do we learn to live in such a way? Through God's teaching us.

Throughout the Bible we read of God teaching His people through His instructions. Sometimes He instructed them by dreams. Other times He instructed them through theophanies (a divine manifestation) or the appearing of angels. At Mount Sinai, He instructed Israel through the Law He gave them. And of course, He instructed them through His prophets who would come with the message, "Thus saith the Lord." What do all these point to? Because of His love for His people, God was instructing them whereby they could glorify Him and enjoy Him. Although there are so many verses that we could examine, three particular passages I want to emphasize. Two I will briefly mention and one I will expound upon.

In Psalm 32, David writes of the blessedness of being forgiven and also of trust in God. Well, what is the basis upon which forgiven people can truly trust in God? It is based on God's promise in Psalm 32:8, "I will instruct you and teach you in the way you should go; I will counsel you with My eye upon you." This is further demonstrated in God's word through the prophet Isaiah. Isaiah 30:18 records the great passage which states that God longs to be gracious to Judah and He waits on high to have compassion toward them. Then, in verse 19 we read of God's promise that He will be gracious to them at the sound of their cry and when He hears it, He will answer. How will God be gracious and compassionate to Judah? Isaiah 30:20-21 gives the answer. "Although the Lord has given you bread of privation and water of oppression, He, your Teacher will no longer hide Himself, but your eyes will behold your Teacher. And your ears will hear a word behind you, 'This is the way, walk in it,' whenever you turn to the right or to the left." Did you notice that even though Judah had been given hard times by the Lord, they would behold Him as their Teacher and He would instruct them in the way they should walk?

Thus, in both Psalm 32:8 and Isaiah 30:20-21 we see that God promises to instruct His people in a particular way. What is the way? It would be the way in which they could glorify Him and enjoy intimacy with Him. What then is the bottom line as to how God instructs His children? He instructs us by His word. And when I speak of His word, I am referring to His written word, the Scriptures. I would never try to put God in a box and say that He would never communicate to someone today in a dream, by an angel, or another way as He did while the Scriptures were being written. At the same time, however, should you believe that God is communicating to you in such a way, you should examine what you have heard next to Scripture for it is authoritative. For example, if you believe you have heard from God by a means other than Scripture and then you find out that it violates Scripture, know that it was not God communicating through that other means because He can never speak contrary to His own word as found in Scripture. And in His Scripture, we can truly be instructed as to how to glorify God and enjoy an intimate relationship with Him.

There is probably no greater passage of Scripture that depicts this than 2 Timothy 3:16-17. I have often referred to Paul's second epistle to Timothy as his deathbed letter as he is awaiting execution at the hands of the Roman government. Usually what someone says on their deathbed is of utmost importance. Throughout this letter Paul states several important truths and principles that Timothy needed to be reminded of and then pass on to others. One of the truths is that in the last days, which both Timothy and we face, difficult times will come. Well, how can we make it through such difficult times? In 2 Timothy 3:14-15, Paul tells Timothy to "continue in the things you have learned and become convinced of" and that from childhood he had "known the sacred writings which are able to give you the wisdom that leads to salvation through faith which is in Christ Jesus." What were the sacred writings? They were the

Old Testament Scriptures. If Timothy was to make it through difficult times and live a godly life even though it meant persecution and even though evil men and impostors would grow progressively worse in their deception, he must continue in the things he had learned from the Scriptures.

Then in verses 16-17, Paul gives the reason why the Scriptures are so important to Timothy then and us today. The Scriptures are profitable for living. In other words, they are profitable for instructing us as to how we can fulfill the chief end for which we were created. Verse 16 starts out, "All Scripture is inspired by God." Whereas the sacred writings of verse 15 would refer to the Old Testament Scriptures, the words "All Scripture" would also include those Scriptures that make up the New Testament. And notice, they are inspired by God. In other words, their source is God. He is the author. J.N.D. Kelly wrote, "The rabbinical teaching was that the Spirit of God rested on and in the prophets and spoke through them so that their words did not come from themselves, but from the mouth of God and they spoke and wrote in the Holy Spirit."[4] Second Peter 1:20-21 also emphasizes this: "But know this first of all, that no prophecy of Scripture is a matter of one's own interpretation, for no prophecy was ever made by an act of human will, but men moved by the Holy Spirit spoke from God." J. Vernon McGee wrote, "The writers of Scripture were not just pens that the Lord picked up and wrote with. The marvel is that God used these men's personalities, expressed things in their thought patterns, yet got through exactly what He wanted to say."[5] As someone has said then, the Bible is "the heart of God in the words of God." And God's heart longs for intimacy with His children.

So, all Scripture is from God and then we see its purpose. It is profitable. As 1 Thessalonians 2:13 tells us, it performs its work in those who believe. And we see there are four things it is profitable for. First of all, it is profitable for teaching or instruction. This really points to teaching us the way God would have us go—the way of righteous living that glorifies God. We saw this previously in Psalm 32:8 and Isaiah 30:20-21. Second, it is profitable for reproof. The word "reproof" means conviction. In Titus 1:9, Paul writes of overseers as "...holding fast the faithful word which is in accordance with the teaching, that he may be able both to exhort in sound doctrine and to refute those who contradict." Yes, the context there speaks of overseers, but any Christian who holds fast to the faithful word will be able to refute those who contradict. Therefore, the Scripture is profitable to refute error and sin. In essence then, it is able to show us where we may have strayed from the way that God has for us. Proverbs 15:31-32 states, "He whose ear listens to the life-giving reproof Will dwell among the wise. He who neglects discipline despises himself, But he who listens to reproof acquires understanding." Where does the life-giving reproof come from? God's written word.

This leads then to the third way in which Scripture is profitable and that is for correction. The word "correction" means restoration to an upright or right state. It refers to an improvement of life or character. The Psalmist wrote in Psalm 119:9, "How can a young man keep his way pure? By keeping it according to Thy word." Do you see how this fits in with reproof? Reproof shows us where we have strayed from the way and when we listen, as we saw in Proverbs 15, then the Scripture is able to correct us and show us how to get back on the way. In other words, restoring us to the way.

Finally, Scripture is profitable for training us in righteousness. The word "training" actually refers to the whole training and education of children. It speaks of a cultivation of the mind and morals. It is also a word that is a synonym for teaching. It usually speaks of concentration on particular skills to fit a person for a desired role.[6] Righteousness means integrity, virtue or purity of life. Thus, Scripture fits a child of God for the desired role of living a righteous life or staying on the way that God has for us.

Then verse 17 tells us the result accomplished when we allow Scripture to do its work in us. When Paul refers to the "man of God" he is speaking of any Christian. Previously, we saw from 1 Thessalonians that the word of God would perform its work in us.

And Micah 2:7de says, "...Do not My words do good To the one walking uprightly?"

Well, the work it performs, the good it does, or the result it accomplishes is that we will be adequate. The word "adequate" means fitted, complete, sufficient, or completely qualified. It refers to the ability to meet the demands, whatever they may be. In other words, whatever God puts in our way. It is in the present tense which speaks of the believer continually being adequate.

What is he adequate for? He is equipped for every good work. The word "equipped" means to furnish perfectly or completely outfit. Fritz Reinecker wrote, "The word was used of documents which were completely outfitted or of a completely outfitted rescue boat."[7] Thus, the Christian, through the Bible, is furnished perfectly for every good or useful work. As 2 Corinthians 9:8 tells us, "And God is able to make all grace abound to you, that always having all sufficiency in everything, you may have an abundance for every good deed..."

Aren't Christians suppose to be involved in good deeds? Paul emphasized this in his epistle to Titus. In Titus 2:14 he wrote of Jesus, "...who gave Himself for us, that He might redeem us from every lawless deed and purify for Himself a people for His own possession, zealous for good deeds." Then in Titus 3:8 he wrote, "This is a trustworthy statement; and concerning these things I want you to speak confidently, so that those who have believed God may be careful to engage in good deeds. These things are good and profitable for men."

Second Timothy 3:16-17 is a definite contrast with what Paul had written in verse 13 concerning the evil men and imposters that proceed from bad to worse as they deceive and are being deceived. Why do they go from bad to worse? They reject the truth of Scripture. Thus, as Titus 1:16 tells us, they may profess to know God, but by their deeds they deny Him and they are worthless for any good deed. The Christian, however, who uses Scripture will be adequate to do any good work that God wants him to do. As J.J. Van Oosterzee writes, "Instruction by the Scripture will secure for every believer continuous, growing, inward capacity and readiness for the accomplishment of every thing pleasing to the Lord."[8] Why should we want to do good works? Matthew 5:16 tells us. "Let your light shine before men in such a way that they may see your good works, and glorify your Father who is in heaven."

Hopefully, we have seen the importance of the Bible, God's written word. It is important in that it gives us the wisdom that leads to salvation through faith which is in Christ Jesus and it is profitable in that it will show us the truths whereby we can grow and be equipped for every good work. I think the importance of the Bible can be summed up in the following quote from *The Treasury of Scripture Knowledge*: "Holy Scripture is the only source of doctrinal and spiritual authority for the Christian. This passage teaches us the sufficiency of Scripture: Scripture furnishes all that the Christian must know to be saved and to grow in grace, and tells us all we need to know to live a life which is pleasing to God. No source of doctrine or revelation outside of Scripture is valid, for such a source would be adding to the written Word of God, which is absolutely forbidden by Scripture."[9]

So, the Bible is a loving Father instructing His children whereby we can live for the purpose for which we were created, to glorify our Father and enjoy Him forever, in this life and throughout eternity.

Our Father, however, also teaches us through example. I mentioned previously that example relates to modeling or imitating a particular action. Who is the example that the Father teaches us through? It is Jesus. The letters "WWJD" (What Would Jesus Do) have become very popular in our day among Christians. I'm afraid, though, that many times we may put that slogan into a list of do's and don'ts much like the Pharisees did with the Law. Rather, we need to focus on what Jesus did when He lived on earth and thus, seek to imitate the heart and attitude that He displayed. Now, before we look at this further, there is something very important we need to realize. No one is ever saved from his sin and brought into relationship with God as a loving Father by seeking to follow Jesus' example. We are saved by trusting in His finished work at Calvary as He died to pay the penalty for our sin. Once we are saved, however, we are to seek to live according to the example of Jesus by the power of the Holy Spirit Who indwells us. Well, what is our Father teaching us through Jesus' example?

I would like to share an experience that Dr. Bruce Waltke mentioned in a lecture during an Old Testament class at Reformed Theological Seminary in Orlando which I believe emphasizes the example of Jesus that we are to learn from. He stated, "A lady decked out with ERA (Equal Rights Amendment) buttons, jewelry (ear-rings, necklace, etc.), and other decor of varying sorts sat down next to me on a plane. I noted in the bag she set down below her seat at least ten different periodicals trumpeting feminist material. Reading her logo, I felt that were I a member of the feminist movement I could have had my devotions reading her. Shortly she turned to me, asking my occupation. Instead of dodging her with identifying myself as a professor of Semitics with a doctorate in Ancient Near Eastern Languages and Literatures, I decided to lance the boil and identify myself as a minister. I got the response I expected. Invectives against the apostle Paul, the Christian faith and the Christian Church for their suppression of women. After she inveighed against the Christian faith in this way for about fifteen minutes she finally allowed me an opportunity to respond. I replied that to a large extent the church was at fault for misrepresenting the teaching of the New Testament. I explained to her that what we mean by male leadership is a leadership of serving those under authority. The heads of the church and of the home serve others in the way that Christ served His church. He gave up His rights to serve, not to be served. I explained that our symbol is not a scepter with which we dominate others but a towel around our waist to wash the feet of those we serve; that the symbol of the church is the cross; that we triumph through humility and a willingness to die for one another as Christ died for His church. As she listened to me and I explained what is meant by a gospel of marriage—that the husband dies for his wife and the wife submits to her husband, as Christ died for His

Teaching Your Children through Instruction and Example

church and the church submits to Him, I noted tears welling up in her eyes. Through tears she said, 'If I could see that, I would throw all this stuff away.' The Gospel of grace touched her heart and healed her wounds." After sharing his experience, Dr. Waltke stated that the life and example of Jesus are summarized in two words. The "towel" and the "cross."

As I reflected on Dr. Waltke's words, I wondered how the word "example" was used of Jesus in the New Testament. In my search I found that there were only two times that the word example was used and they were in connection with the towel and the cross. John 13 records Jesus washing the feet of the disciples. Verse 2 states that He was demonstrating the full extent of His love for them (NIV). Of course, washing feet was the responsibility of the lowest slave. In John 13:14-15 Jesus states, "If I then, the Lord and Teacher, washed your feet, you also ought to wash one another's feet. For I gave you an example that you also should do as I did to you." Did you notice that Jesus described Himself as the Teacher and He taught His disciples by His example of love through servanthood? Then Peter writes in 1 Peter 2:21-24, "For you have been called for this purpose, since Christ also suffered for you, leaving you an example for you to follow in His steps, WHO COMMITTED NO SIN, NOR WAS ANY DECEIT FOUND IN HIS MOUTH; and while being reviled, He did not revile in return; while suffering, He uttered no threats, but kept entrusting Himself to Him who judges righteously; and He Himself bore our sins in His body on the cross, that we might die to sin and live to righteousness." Jesus' death on the cross not only purchased our salvation, but in the process of His suffering at the cross, He gave us an example for when we face suffering that we may follow in His steps.

An excellent commentary which summarizes these two passages is found in Philippians 2:5-11. Paul states that Jesus emptied Himself by taking the form of a bond-servant and being made in the likeness of men. He also humbled Himself as He was obedient to experiencing death on a cross. Dr. Waltke describes this as "Jesus disadvantaging Himself for the advantage of others." That characterizes true servanthood. There is one very important truth that we must never forget as Jesus lived out true servanthood. He never complained. And as Paul wrote in Philippians 2:5, that is the attitude we are to have. In other words, the example we are to follow.

In John 10:10, Jesus states that He came that we might experience abundant living as He did while He was on earth. In fact, Jesus lived the most abundant life that a person could ever experience. And what characterized His life? He delighted to do the Father's will which was being a bond-servant and through His servanthood He glorified His Father and enjoyed an intimate relationship with Him. Our loving Father wants His children to experience this abundant life also. That is the purpose behind His teaching us through instruction and example as displayed in His Son.

Earthly parents should have a similar desire for their own children. Unfortunately, the world's view of abundant living is just the opposite of God's view and parents can so easily get caught up in trying to assist their children to obtain the abundant life that the world seeks to offer rather than the abundant life through following Jesus. And such can lead to dangerous consequences.

The importance of parents teaching their children through instruction and example was depicted in a sermon I heard back in the early 1980's. The pastor was asking how there could be such a minimal influence of Christianity in the Middle East today when it was so vibrant in that area as recorded in the book of Acts and in a few later centuries. In other words, some of the churches mentioned in the New Testament no longer exist. How could that be? He stated that he felt that it was the failure of not faithfully teaching the next generation. Then he challenged the congregation by stating that we needed to realize that America was only one generation away from there being no Christian witness in our country. What a frightening thought that is. We are already seeing this to a degree because there are some children in America who have no idea what the real meaning of Christmas is and thus, just know the name "Jesus" as a curse word. We have a Scriptural example of this. Judges 2:7 records that the people of Israel served the LORD all the days of Joshua and all the days of the elders who survived Joshua. Joshua and his generation had seen all the great work that the LORD had done for Israel. Judges 2:10b states, however, "and there arose another generation after them who did not know the LORD, nor yet the work which He had done for Israel." What did this generation do then? They did evil, served the Baals, forsook the LORD and followed the gods of the people around them. In other words, they sought abundant life through following worldly gods. Did such bring abundant life? Not at all. Rather, it led to bondage at the hands of their enemies. If that happened to Israel then, it can happen to us today.

Well, how can parents avoid making the same mistake Israel made? It is Christian parents taking seriously their responsibility to faithfully teach their children the truths of God's word. Yes, we are thankful for such things as Sunday Schools, Vacation Bible Schools, Children's ministries and Christian schools, but they are not to be the primary source of our children's religious and moral education. That is the responsibility and privilege of the parents. Christians are often challenged with our mission from Christ which we refer to as "The Great Commission" of going and making disciples of all nations, teaching them to observe all that He had commanded (Matthew 28:19-20). Well, "The Great Commission" should begin in the home with the parents seeking to make disciples of their children. As Dr. James Dobson stated, "According to the Christian values that govern my life, my most important reason for living is to get...the gospel safely in the hands of my children. Of course, I want to place it in as many other hands as possible; nevertheless, my number one responsibility is to evangelize my own children. I hope millions of other fathers agree with that ultimate priority."[10] The importance of this truth is taught throughout the Bible.

Let's emphasize only a couple of the many passages that depict this truth. In Deuteronomy 4:1, we read that God was teaching Israel to perform His statutes and judgments. And what would be the result of obeying them? Israel would live and go in and take possession of the Promised Land. In other words, they would experience abundant living. But what else were they to do? As verse

9 tells us, they were to give heed to themselves and keep their soul diligently so that they would not forget what their eyes had seen and that it would not depart from their hearts so that they could make them known to their sons and grandsons. Then in verse 10, Moses reminds Israel of when they were at Horeb and heard His words so that they would fear Him and teach their children.

This responsibility for parents is further displayed in Deuteronomy 6:4-9 which is known as the "Shema." God tells Israel that they are to love Him with all their heart, soul and might. And the words which He was commanding them, they were to be on their hearts and then teach them diligently to their children.

From both of these passages there are several important principles that parents need to be aware of in order to properly teach their children. First, as with discipline, both parents are to be involved in teaching their children through instruction. In Proverbs 1:8 and Proverbs 6:20, children are told to hear and observe the instruction, commandment and teaching of both parents. In reality, the mother is especially important to the religious and moral education of her children. We have examples of this throughout the Bible. Proverbs 31:1 speaks of the words of King Lemuel which he had been taught by his mother. Earlier in the chapter I mentioned 2 Timothy 3:14-15 in which Paul exhorted Timothy to continue in the things he had learned and the sacred writings which he had known from childhood. Well, who taught Timothy? In 2 Timothy 1:5, Paul wrote of the sincere faith of Timothy's grandmother, Lois, and his mother, Eunice. Timothy's father was a Greek and his mother was a Jew. He obviously didn't get any religious instruction or training from his father, but he did from his mother. Hopefully this will encourage mothers today. Yes, God's intention is for both parents to be involved in the religious instruction of the children, but there are many homes today in which only one parent is a committed Christian. And in so many cases, that parent is the mother. Then there are single parent homes in which more often than not the mother is the one who really raises the children. Mothers, if you are alone in teaching your children, don't be discouraged. With your heavenly Father's help, you can be like Eunice to Timothy. In fact, John Wesley stated, "I learned more about Christianity from my mother than from all the theologians in England."[11]

A second principle that parents should be aware of in order to effectively instruct their children is that they should seek to continually study and learn from God's word themselves. Our Father taught me this several years ago through my grandmother, Cokie. It was the fall of 1991 and the family was preparing to celebrate my grandmother's 90th birthday. Unfortunately, she got sick and had to be hospitalized for an extended period. I went to my hometown of Chattanooga, Tennessee to visit my grandmother in the hospital. We really didn't know if she would ever get well and be allowed to go home. While in Chattanooga, I asked my mother if one evening I could have a few minutes alone with Cokie. I was extremely close to Cokie and I could write countless pages of special times that I shared with her and my grandfather. I must be honest, though, that there were none more special than this night because of what she taught me. As I talked with her about what she was facing, possibly even death, I shared with her several promises from God's word. I will never forget her response. She said, "I need to memorize those promises." Imagine that. Cokie was almost 90 years old and not sure of how much longer she would be living, but she was still interested in learning truths from God's word. This experience really spoke to me in that I should never be content where I was spiritually and realize there was always more I could learn. So, if parents want to instruct their children from the word of God, they need to continually learn themselves.

A third principle for parents as they seek to instruct their children involves what they are to teach their children. As we saw in Deuteronomy 4:1,9-10, they should teach God's statutes and judgments. They should also teach them to learn to fear or reverence God. From Deuteronomy 6:4-5 we read that parents should teach doctrine to their children such as the LORD is one. And they should be taught to seek to love the LORD their God with their total being, heart, soul, and might. This really addresses a challenge that

Christian parents face in America, which is much different than in other countries of the world, especially third world countries. Unfortunately, in America we often compartmentalize our lives. For example, there may be the occupation compartment, the family compartment, the social compartment, the athletic compartment, the financial compartment, the education compartment, the recreational compartment and the religious compartment just to mention a few. Thus, so many Christians only associate a commitment to Jesus as it relates to the religious compartment and don't see Him as having any influence in the rest of their lives. If parents instruct their children in that way rather than instructing them that Jesus is to affect every aspect of life, they have failed to properly instruct their children.

A beautiful commentary on these two passages is Psalm 78 written by Asaph. He wrote in verses 1-8:

> "Listen, O my people, to my instruction; Incline your ears to the words of my mouth. I will open my mouth in a parable; I will utter dark sayings of old, Which we have heard and known, And our fathers have told us. We will not conceal them from their children, But tell to the generation to come the praises of the LORD, And His strength and His wondrous works that He has done. For He established a testimony in Jacob, And appointed a law in Israel, Which He commanded our fathers, That they should teach them to their children, That the generation to come might know, even the children yet to be born, That they may arise and tell them to their children, That they should put their confidence in God, And not forget the works of God, But keep His commandments, And not be like their fathers, a stubborn and rebellious generation, A generation that did not prepare its heart, And whose spirit was not faithful to God."

Did you notice all that should be taught to our children just from those few verses? The praises of the LORD. His strength and wondrous works. His law. That their confidence should be in God

Teaching Your Children through Instruction and Example

and not forget His works. Keep His commandments and learn from the failure of their fathers.

Another way that parents were to instruct their children was through memorial stones which were a reminder of God's faithfulness. Parents today can establish their own memorial stones as a teaching device to remind their children of God's faithfulness. And we must never forget that the Bible is full of countless stories of faithful and unfaithful people, which can be used to teach valuable truths and principles. The great preacher, G. Campbell Morgan, stated: "My dedication to the preaching of the Word was maternal… when but eight years old I preached to my little sister and to her dolls arrayed in orderly form before me. My sermons were Bible stories which I had first heard from my mother."[12] Here again, parents need to be continuously learning these truths and principles themselves whereby they can effectively teach them to their children. What, though, is the purpose of all that we teach our children from the Bible? It is, as we saw previously from 2 Timothy 3:15, that we will teach the wisdom that leads to salvation through faith which is in Christ Jesus and that He will affect every aspect (compartment) of their lives.

A final principle for parents to be conscious of as they instruct their children is that they are to take every opportunity possible to teach. What did we see in Deuteronomy 6:7? To teach God's word to their children when they are sitting in their house or when they walk by the way or when they lie down or rise up. If we really believe that the Bible addresses every area of our lives, then there are numerous opportunities for parents to teach their children from daily experiences. And we must never forget that such instruction should begin early in the life of a child. As stated in the previous chapter, we can teach our children through discipline before instruction, but instruction should not be far behind. As Arthur Jackson wrote, "It is common sense to put the seal on the wax while it is soft."[13] I once saw on a news program a Middle Eastern Muslim mother asking her 3½ year old daughter, "Do you like Jews?" to which the daughter responded, "No." Then she asked, "What are

Jews?" to which the daughter responded, "They are apes and pigs." Obviously this mother had taken every opportunity early in her daughter's life to teach her to hate Jews. I heard on the same newscast a Muslim father saying, "I have a son and I am preparing him for martyrdom." The young son asked his father, "If I blow myself up, will I get a new car and rifle?" The father replied, "Son, if you blow yourself up, you will get everything you want." Such teaching to young children at every opportunity, even though it's a lie, has led to the numerous suicide bombings in Israel and the killing of many Jews. Jeremiah Burroughs' words of several hundred years ago are so appropriate here. "There is little hope for children who are educated wickedly. If the dye is in the wool, it is hard to get it out of the cloth."[14] Christian parents, if such parents as these Muslim parents take every opportunity to instruct their children early and often in lies, shouldn't we take every opportunity to instruct our children early and often in the truth? T. Dewitt Talmage wrote,

> "I tell you, my friends, the reason we don't reclaim all our children from worldliness is because we begin too late. Parents wait until their children lie before they teach them the value of truth. They wait until their children swear before they teach them the importance of righteous conversation. They wait until their children are all wrapped up in this world before they tell them of a better world. Too late with your prayers. Too late with your discipline. Too late with your benediction. You put all care upon your children between 12 and 18. Why do you not put the chief care between 4 and 9? It is too late to repair a vessel when it has got out of the dry-dock!"[15]

So, parents are to be involved in teaching their children through instruction, but just as important, if not more important, is to teach them through our example. In other words, our children need to see us living out those Biblical truths we are instructing them. In Matthew 23, Jesus exposed the Pharisees for their hypocrisy. He told the multitudes and His disciples in verse 3, "all that they tell you, do and observe, but do not do according to their deeds; for they say things, and do not do them." Consequently, the Pharisees, when they would speak from God's word, would be saying truths that the people ought to do and observe. The problem, however, was they did not practice what they taught. A modern day equivalent of that is the phrase, "Do as I say, not as I do." If our children don't see us seeking to practice what we instruct them, then chances are they will do as we do rather than as we say.

My mother sent me a cartoon from a church bulletin, which depicts this truth. On the wall of a house is the saying, "Home Sweet Home." Then the husband is pictured arguing with his wife and in turn, you see the small son arguing with the cat. The caption reads, "Parents...remember that children will probably follow your example rather than your advice." As John Locke wrote, "Parents wonder why the streams are bitter, when they themselves have poisoned the fountain."[16] And how do we so often poison the fountain of our children? Through our example of not living what we instruct our children. Of course, we will never be perfect in our example. Jesus is the only perfect example, but we are to seek to be consistent in our example.

Earlier in this chapter we saw from Isaiah 30:21 that the Lord our Teacher would tell His people, "This is the way, walk in it." Well, by our example, parents should be saying to their children, "This is the way, walk in it." Cotton Mather wrote, "If we teach good things, it is hopeful that they will be learned. If our lives exemplify virtue, it is hopeful that they will be imitated."[17]

Several years ago I heard an alarming and disturbing statistic. A large percentage of abused children grow up to be child abusers. I couldn't believe that when I first heard it, but really this depicts a truth from Scripture. In Luke 6:40, Jesus stated, "A pupil is not above his teacher; but everyone, after he has been fully trained, will be like his teacher." Abused children who grow up to be child abusers are just imitating what they have been taught by the example of their teacher, the parent(s) that abused them. This leads to a very important question that parents should ask themselves. What am I teaching my children through the example they see in the practice of my daily life? The following poem to fathers, but would apply to both parents, depicts how vital is the example that we are to set before our children.

> There are little eyes upon you, and
> they're watching night and day;
> There are little ears that quickly
> take in every word you say;
> There are little hands all eager to
> do everything you do.
> And a little boy who's dreaming of
> the day he'll be just like you.
> You're the little fellow's idol. You're
> the wisest of the wise;
> In his little mind, about you no
> suspicions ever rise.
> He believes in you devoutly, holds
> that all you say and do.
> He will say and do in your way
> when he's grown up like you.
> This wide-eyed fellow who
> believes you're always right.
> And his ears always open and
> he watches day and night.
> You are setting an example every
> day in all you do.
> For the little fellow who's waiting
> to grow up to be just like you.[18]

In October 1811, Samuel Worcester preached a sermon entitled, "Parental Duties Illustrated." Part of that sermon is so important to this principle. He stated, "In proportion to our faith and piety, we shall be unceasing and abundant in our prayers, our instructions and admonitions, that they may be brought to renounce the vanities of the world and set their hope in God. But, my brethren, if we are not religious ourselves, how can we discharge our duty to our children. If we do not walk in our houses with a perfect heart, how can we command our children and our households after us to keep the way of the Lord? If we do not live habitually in the fear of the Lord, if we do not live, as the grace of God which brings salvation teaches, in the denial of ungodliness and worldly lusts, soberly, righteously, and devoutly in the world, how can we expect to train our children in the way they should go, so that when they are old they will not depart from it?"[19]

Worcester's words remind me of another poem that I learned years ago when I was being discipled by another man.

> "You're writing a gospel, a chapter each day,
> by the deeds that you do and the words that you say.
> Men read what you write-distorted or true;
> What is the gospel according to you?"[20]

Parents, what is the gospel that our children are reading as they observe our lives? I once witnessed a conversation between a lady and a teenage boy before a church service. The teenager made a certain request of the lady to which the lady then stated to him, "You are just like your father." Upon hearing this, the teenager abruptly replied in a very negative tone, "No, I'm not like my father." His response spoke volumes about their relationship and made me wonder what was the example and the gospel that this father had displayed before his teenage son that the son didn't want to be compared to his father.

The contrast of that young man's statement is a statement written by Dan Smith II about his father. I was once in a patio furniture store and noticed a plaque on the wall. This plaque had on it a couple of pictures of Dan and his father, the store manager, standing side by side. It also had on it Psalm 118:24 which was Mr. Smith's favorite Bible verse. The final thing on it was Dan's statement. It read, "My success in life will not depend on fame or fortune, but whether I can touch someone's life the way my father touched mine." I had already finished this book and was having it edited, but after reading Dan's statement, I had to include it because it so depicted the principle of parents teaching their children through example. I called the store to talk with Mr. Smith. I told him I had bought some furniture at his store. He may have thought I was calling to complain about something in reference to the furniture. I told him, however, that I wasn't calling about the furniture, but about the plaque on the wall. Mr. Smith enjoyed talking about furniture, but even more so there was an excitement as he talked about the plaque. You will understand why in just a moment. I related to Mr. Smith that Dan's statement had so impressed me that I wanted to include it in this book. Mr. Smith then shared with me the story behind the plaque. It was a birthday present from Dan. Dan had graduated from the University of Central Florida with straight A's and was going to law school at the University of Florida. Finances were tight and with his father's birthday approaching he didn't have much money to get a gift. So, the plaque was given as an expression of love and appreciation to his father for the love and example he had been to Dan. As Mr. Smith told me about this gift, I had chill bumps and he stated that he still tears up when he looks at this special gift from his son. To use the words of a commercial of a major credit card, the gift was "priceless" to Mr. Smith. Whereas the son's response in the previous paragraph was as if it were an insult to say he was like his father, Dan's statement depicts that for him, one of the greatest compliments you could give him was that he was just like his father.

Previously I mentioned the example of servanthood that Jesus lived out to those under His authority. We know that the Bible teaches that children are to obey their parents in the Lord for this is right (Ephesians 6:1), but we see so much rebellion against parental authority by young people today. With all this rebellion among young people in our society today, it has made me wonder that if our children saw in their parents the example of servanthood displayed by Jesus, would there be as much rebellion? Personally, I don't think so.

Let me share with you a few examples of what I mean. Two are positive and one is negative. I have a friend who had a son who

Teaching Your Children through Instruction and Example

played college baseball. His son needed some surgery which was essential to his playing his best. Yes, he could have got the surgery done in the city where they lived by a competent surgeon, but this father made the special effort to go out of state and get a real specialist to do the surgery. Consequently, this father's effort involved added expense and time away from work, but he was displaying servanthood to his son and it really ministered to the son.

A second example involves a couple a few years older than I. They have two daughters who have gone through some difficult circumstances. This couple have been real servants to their daughters spiritually, emotionally, financially and in many other ways. I must add that the dad is actually a step-dad to the girls but they see him as their true dad through his support and servanthood to them which they've never received from their biological father. Now, you may say, wouldn't most parents do the same thing for their children as these two examples? Probably so, but there could be a big difference in the attitude displayed. Previously, I stated that in Jesus' servanthood He never complained. Parents may often display servanthood to their children but in the process complain about it in subtle ways which does not depict true servanthood. Such statements as: "Do you know how much this is going to cost me and it is going to mess up or ruin my life?" or "This is a waste of my time when I could be doing other things," or "I hope you appreciate the sacrifice I'm making for you," are a few examples of complaining that depict to our children that we don't want to display servanthood to them. Such statements are very unloving and can be very devastating to our children. They really depict an attitude displayed by Jephthah as recorded in the book of Judges. In Judges 11, Jephthah makes a tragic vow that if the LORD would give him victory over the Ammonites, then whatever comes out of the door of his house upon his return, he would offer as a burnt offering to the LORD (Judges 11:30-31). Sadly, when he returned home, his only child, a daughter, was the first one to come out of the door. What was his response? "Alas, my daughter! You have brought me very low, and you are among those who trouble me; for I have given my word to the LORD, and I cannot take it back" (Judges 11:35). Did you notice his attitude? He was the one who made the rash vow, but tells his daughter that she was the one who had brought him very low and troubled him. Why? As Dr. Waltke wrote, "She kept him from his full potential as leader. He does not think of what her death meant to her but to him. She brought him down so that his family could not continue."[21] He was more concerned about himself than his daughter, which is the opposite of servanthood. Basically, he was saying to her, "You have ruined my life."

This is further illustrated in the third example. There was a young boy who went to his mother before school one morning asking her if she would iron him another shirt for the shirt he was wearing was very uncomfortable. The mother had to quickly leave for an important business meeting but the father was still at home. So, she told her young son to go to his father and ask him. The son replied that he would just wear the shirt he had on. The son was afraid to ask his father to serve him in this way because of the negative response that he expected from his father for such a request. So, the mother displayed servanthood to her son by ironing another shirt even though she had to leave for an important meeting. And when we display true servanthood to our children, we are writing a gospel for them to read which imitates Jesus and His example.

Christians, we have a loving Father who is very interested in our lives and the way we live. He wants us to live an abundant, fulfilled life through a continual, intimate relationship with Him. Consequently, He has instructed us through His word and the perfect example of Jesus to teach us how to live such a life. Parents, we should have the same concern for our children. We should want them to have the most abundant life possible, but let's never forget that the world's view of abundant living is much different from God's view as we saw previously from the Westminster Confession. Parents, if we want our children to know how to experience such a life, we need to teach them through instruction from God's word and then by our example as we live out those Biblical truths before their very eyes.

Chapter Seven

Demonstrating Grace and Compassion to Your Children

And He said, "A certain man had two sons; and the younger of them said to his father, 'Father, give me the share of the estate that falls to me.' And he divided his wealth between them. And not many days later, the younger son gathered everything together and went on a journey into a distant country, and there he squandered his estate with loose living. Now when he had spent everything, a severe famine occurred in that country, and he began to be in need. And he went and attached himself to one of the citizens of that country, and he sent him into the fields to feed swine. And he was longing to fill his stomach with the pods that the swine were eating, and no one was giving anything to him. But when he came to his senses, he said, 'How many of my father's hired men have more than enough bread, but I am dying here with

> hunger! I will get up and go to my father, and will say to him, "Father, I have sinned against heaven, and in your sight; I am no longer worthy to be called your son; make me as one of your hired men."' And he got up and came to his father. But while he was still a long way off, his father saw him, and felt compassion for him, and ran and embraced him, and kissed him. And the son said to him, 'Father, I have sinned against heaven, and in your sight; I am no longer worthy to be called your son.' But the father said to his slaves, 'Quickly bring out the best robe and put it on him, and put a ring on his hand and sandals on his feet; and bring the fattened calf, kill it, and let us eat and be merry; for this son of mine was dead, and has come to life again; he was lost, and has been found.' And they began to be merry.
>
> —Luke 15:11-24

One of the most beloved of Jesus' parables is found in Luke 15. We often refer to it as "The Parable of the Prodigal Son." I had rather refer to it as "The Parable of the Gracious and Compassionate Father." The father is referred to at least 12 times in this parable. This parable is recorded in Luke 15:11-32 and we see the father dealing with his two sons. For the purposes of this chapter, however, we only want to focus our attention on verses 11-24 and the father's dealing with the younger son, the prodigal. Before we look at the parable in detail, we need to understand it within the context. In verses 1-2, the Pharisees and scribes were upset that tax-gatherers and sinners were coming to listen to Jesus. The Babylonian Talmud stated that rabbis did not eat with such people because they did not keep the law in the same way that the Pharisees did.[1] Thus, verse 3 tells us that Jesus told them this parable. And the word "parable" is singular even though He tells them three parables in this chapter. That is because there is one central theme in each of

Demonstrating Grace and Compassion to Your Children

the parables—the grace of God, which results in joy in heaven. G. Campbell Morgan sees these three parables as really three phases of one parable. There was the story of a shepherd, a woman and a father. The emphasis of the first parable is the shepherd who is willing to suffer in order to find the lost sheep. The second parable emphasizes the woman searching for the lost coin. The final parable emphasizes the father singing at the return of the lost son. Thus, each parable is concerned with something that is lost and then restored which results in overwhelming joy and celebration.[2] So, as we look at this great parable, hopefully parents will learn from our heavenly Father the importance of demonstrating grace and compassion to their children.

Jesus starts out the parable by stating a certain man had two sons. The younger son came to him and wanted to lay claim to his share of the estate. According to Scripture, fathers at times would give gifts to their children while the father was still alive. When a father would give a gift, he normally gave the capital or property, but retained the income from it.[3] In other words, the capital would belong to the child(ren) and the father would receive interest from it. If the child decided to sell the capital, the buyer would not gain possession of it until the father's death.[4] This would continue to provide for the father until his death. According to the law of Deuteronomy 21:27, the older son would receive two-thirds of the estate and the younger son would receive one-third.

In this parable, however, the younger son wanted now what should have only been his after his father's death. Thus, what the son did would have been totally disrespectful to his father. Why? In essence, he was saying to his father, "I want you dead." It is important to understand what the typical father in the Middle Eastern culture would have done at such a request. He would have slapped the boy across the face and driven him out of the house. This son made a request that was unthinkable and would have been denied.[5] Yet, Jesus tells us that the father divided the estate between the two sons. As we examine this parable we are going to see several things that the father did which are uncharacteristic of a father in that culture. Now, as shown by the celebration that is mentioned in later verses, this father was obviously very wealthy. He was probably well respected in the community and if he gave a banquet, the community would respond to his invitation.[6] It would appear that the older son did with his share of the inheritance what was previously described. He allowed the father to receive the income from the estate. The younger son did totally the opposite.

In verse 13 we read three things that his younger son did. First, in just a few days he gathered everything together from his share of the estate. This means that he took his one-third of the inheritance and converted it all to cash. Here again, it's important to understand the significance of this in light of the culture. With the son selling his share of the inheritance, his attitude toward his father became public knowledge. Thus, the family is shamed within the entire community. The mention of his selling his share of the estate within a few days was probably the result of the anger that would be felt for him because he had shamed his father.[7] The community would reject him. Why? It was the custom of that day for children to stay and care for their aging parents. The sons were to make sure that their fathers were buried properly and that mothers were cared for until their death. So, the actions of this son showed total disregard for his parents.

According to the Jewish Talmud, at the time of Jesus, Jews had a method of punishing a Jewish boy who had lost the family inheritance to Gentiles. It was called the "qetsatsah ceremony." If a Jewish boy lost the inheritance to the Gentiles, and later returned home, he would face this ceremony. At this ceremony the people of the village would have a large earthen jar filled with burned nuts and burned corn. Then, in the presence of the boy they would break the jar. As they were doing this, the community would shout, "So and so is cut off from his people." From that point on they would have nothing to do with the boy. He was cut off and shunned in their eyes and thus, considered dead. This is much more serious than the shunning that takes place within the Amish community. When the Amish shun a person, that person can still eat at a separate table, but with the Jewish ceremony just described there would be no contact whatsoever with the boy.[8]

The second thing the younger son did was to go on a journey into a distant or foreign country. It appears he wanted freedom from his father and wanted as far away as he could go. As Fredric Godet wrote, "Two things impel to act thus: the air of the paternal home oppresses him, he feels the constraint of his father's presence; then the world without attracts him, he hopes to enjoy himself. But to realize his wishes, he needs two things-freedom and money. Here is the image of a heart swayed by licentious appetites; God is the obstacle in its way, and freedom to do anything appears to it as the condition of happiness."[9] So, the distant country speaks of a love for the world which 1 John 2:16 describes as the lust of the flesh, the lust of the eyes and the boastful pride of life.

Finally, the son squandered his estate with loose or riotous living. What had taken his father so long to accumulate was squandered in a short time. The word "squandered" means to scatter abroad or disperse. It was used of throwing grain a considerable distance up into the air whereby it could be separated from the chaff. We're not told exactly how he squandered the estate but he wasted it to satisfy his selfish desires.

In verses 14-16, Jesus speaks of the condition the son found himself in after squandering his share of the estate. He had spent everything and a severe famine hit the country that he was in. Obviously, if he had been a wise steward, the famine may not have affected him, but he had spent it all and when the famine came, he was in extreme need. He had so wasted his estate on his wants, that when the famine came, he couldn't even meet his needs. There is something very important that we need to consider here. I'm sure that he had many friends that helped him squander his estate with loose living. Where were these friends, though, when he had nothing and was in need? They were no where to be found. Doesn't this show us that the indulgence of sinful pleasures and passions ends in anything but happiness?[10] Norval Geldenhays wrote, "When a man has sacrificed his life on the idolatrous altars of pleasures and selfishness in the far country, he is cruelly disillusioned by realizing that this distant land has nothing to offer in lieu of the precious treasures he has wasted there; in his innermost being he is left impoverished and starved."[11]

So, what did he do? Verse 15 gives the answer. He attaches himself to a citizen of that country who in turn sends the son into the fields to feed the swine. The word "attached" means to glue together or to cement or to fasten firmly. In other words, he forced himself on a citizen of the country. Let's reflect on this as it relates to the culture. Remember what he was facing if he went home. The qetsatsah ceremony. Thus, it appears that he may have been trying to earn back the money so that he could go home. Well, what did the citizen have him do? He was given the most despicable occupation known to the Jews. He was sent into the fields to feed the swine. Thus, he was totally humiliated. Not only was he totally humiliated, but he was totally desperate. Verse 16 tells us that he was longing to fill his stomach with the pods that the swine were eating. The word "pods" refers to the little horn-shaped parts of the carob tree. There was a substance inside these pods with a sweet taste. They were used to feed the swine and also for food for the lower classes.[12] To the Jews this was the poorest type of food possible.

We also read in verse 16 that he could not even get anyone to feed him these pods. So, he was even lower than the lowest class of people and even lower than the pigs. The pigs were of more value than he in that famined country. The rabbis of that day would have considered this being in the direst need.[13] He may have felt like the Psalmist in Psalm 142:4, "Look to the right and see; For there is no one who regards me; There is no escape for me; No one cares for my soul." There was a Jewish saying, "When Israel is reduced to the carob tree, they become repentant."[14] Truly, that is the case for this young man.

Consequently, in verses 17-19, Jesus speaks of the son's repentance. You notice that he came to his senses. In other words, he reflected on all that had happened. He saw his real condition. What did that cause him to realize? First, that his father's hired men had plenty of bread to eat while he was perishing with hunger. Second, he realized that the house of his father was not only sufficient, but it was a house of superabundance and wealth. Most importantly, however, he realized that his actions were sin and he needed to go to his father and confess. So, he determines what to say. He would first say, "Father, I have sinned against heaven, and in your sight." It is important to realize that the son's sorrow was not for what he had lost, but what he had done. He had sinned. The word "sinned" means to miss the mark in that he had missed or wandered from the path of uprightness. He also recognizes that his sin is first against God, represented by the word "heaven." After being confronted by Nathan, David recognized this truth even though he had sinned against Bathsheba and Uriah with his adultery and murder for he wrote in Psalm 51:4, "Against Thee, Thee only, I have sinned, And done what is evil in Thy sight, So that Thou are justified when Thou dost speak, And blameless when Thou dost judge." The young son also recognized that he had sinned against his father. The main thing about this son's sin was not that he had squandered his inheritance, but that he had rebelled against love. Consequently, verse 19 tells us how he feels about himself. This is demonstrated in that he says further, "I am no longer worthy to be called your son; make me as one of your hired men." The word "worthy" means one who has merited anything worthy. When he speaks of the father's hired men, we must realize what he is saying. In that part of the world one did not hire a teacher or even a regular full-time servant. You only hire a day laborer. Thus, he was saying, "Treat me as one who is hired daily." Day laborers were lower than ordinary slaves because they could be dismissed at a day's notice while ordinary slaves were in some respects considered a part of the family.[15] The son then, had no hope for immediate and full restoration.[16] He was much like the tax-gatherer in Luke 18 who stood some distance away in the Temple. Isn't this a contrast with his attitude as depicted in verses 12-13? Pride and arrogance versus humility and a contrite heart. In pride he wanted what shouldn't have been his until after his father's death. In humility he was willing to take the position of the lowest slave and obey his father as a servant would his master.

Now we get to the key part of this parable and that is the grace and compassion of the father, as found in verses 20-24. Verse 20 tells us that the son gets up and returns to his father. This verse also tells us five very important things about the father. First, the father was looking for his son. Yes, to the citizens of the village the son was forgotten and shunned. Not to the father, however. I imagine that every day he went to the gate of the city looking off in the direction in which his son had gone, with a longing for him to return. He never gave up hope. What does this show us? When a child is lost like this son, who suffers the most, the child or the parents? While the son was living the riotous life, he could have cared less about the father, but the father was grieving over his son. Why did he grieve so much? Because he loved the son and wanted the joy associated with the relationship of a father and son. The father wanted the son back even more than the son wanted to come back. The son only thought about the father when he came to his senses. His love for the father had grown cold. The father, on the other hand, never stopped thinking about the son and his love never grew cold.

Yes, the son eventually wanted to come back, but can't you imagine his fear? What would happen? To the citizens of the distant country, he was lower than the pigs. To the citizens of the village, he would be facing the shame associated with the qetsatsah ceremony. What about his father?

One day, off in the distance, the father saw his son coming. Of course, the distance is more spiritual than physical.[17] What did the father do then? Did he go back to his house and wait for the son to crawl back begging for forgiveness? Did he want the son to be humiliated further in front of the citizens? No. The second thing he did then was he felt compassion for his son. In other words, he was moved to pity. That is the attitude of a gracious father.

So, the father felt compassion but he also demonstrated that compassion as shown by the third thing he did. He ran to his son. It was undignified for an elderly man to run in public. To do so was considered humiliating.[18] Yet, he did just that because it was his son. Let's not forget that the father would know how the village would react to the son's return. The father then wants to reach his son before the son reaches the village. He knows that if there is a reconciliation with his son in public, then none of the villagers will treat him badly and will not even suggest that the qetsatsah ceremony take place. I can imagine that the son was walking slowly, but the father was running, even though the people would look down upon that. Charles Spurgeon wrote, "The prodigal son was resolved to come, yet he was half-afraid. But we read that the father ran. Slow are the steps of repentance, but swift are the feet of forgiveness. God can run where we can scarcely limp, and if we are limping toward Him, He will run toward us. Though the father was out of breath, he was not out of love."[19] And Joseph Alleine wrote, "O the haste that mercy makes: the sinner makes not half that speed. I think I see how his heart moves, how his compassions yearn. How quick-sighted is love!"[20]

This is further illustrated by the fourth thing the father did. He embraced his son. The word "embraced" actually means to fall on his neck. It is important to realize that the father embraced his son who smelled like a pig. He was filthy. That didn't matter to the father. His son was home. Finally, the father kissed his son. The word "kissed" here means to kiss and kiss again. In Scripture, to kiss fervently is a sign of forgiveness. David did this to Absalom for 2 Samuel 14:33 states, "So when Joab came to the king and told him, he called for Absalom. Thus he came to the king and prostrated himself on his face to the ground before the king, and the king kissed Absalom." Do you realize what the father is saying to his son? "You are forgiven, regardless of what you have done. I love you." As Kenneth Bailey wrote, "The father does not demonstrate love in response to his son's confession. Rather, out of his own compassion he empties himself, assumes the form of a servant, and runs to reconcile his estranged son."[21] Here again, let's relate this to the culture. If such had occurred in that culture, the father would have been expected to sit in isolation in his house waiting upon the son to hear what the son had to say. It would have been the mother that would have run to the son and kissed him.²² As stated before, in Scripture God is often presented as a father who displays the tender compassion of a mother. As we saw in chapter 3 from Isaiah 66:13a, "As one whom his mother comforts, so I will comfort you." Let's understand what Jesus is doing here. He was basically asking the Pharisees, "Would you blame a father for doing such for a repenting son?" Of course, they shouldn't. Well then, what is wrong with God receiving repentant sinners? Thankfully, nothing is wrong with it or else we would all be lost forever.

You may have noticed that the father did all this even before the son could say anything. So, in verse 21, the son says part of what he had planned to say. "Father, I have sinned against heaven and in your sight; I am no longer worthy to be called your son." We see, however, that the son did not have time to say, "make me as one of your hired men." Why? The father interrupted him. What is significant about this? I believe it is this. I believe the son came back feeling like he would have to earn back his father's love and how would he best earn it? By performance or service as a hired man. Maybe he felt that he needed to earn back the money he had squandered. That was not the feeling of the father, however. The son came back afraid, but the perfect love of the father would cast out all fear. The father's actions in verses 22-24 demonstrate that he didn't want performance. He wanted the father-son relationship, a relationship of love. The son, from his perspective, felt that he was no longer worthy to be called his father's son. But the father demonstrates to his son that he sees him as worthy. That is grace. The son's worth in the father's eyes is not based on his performance. His worth is based on the fact that he is the son of his father. Remember, the father ran to his son. What is significant about that? As they walked from the city gate through the village to get back to the house, the father was willing to walk with his son to protect him against any humiliation from the citizens of the village.

Next, the father calls for a celebration, a banquet. Let's not forget what the son may have been fearful of facing. The qetsatsah ceremony. What a contrast! A possible shunning ceremony versus a celebration. Thus, the father tells the slaves to quickly bring out the best robe. He didn't tell the son to get cleaned up whereby he would look respectable. His dirty son was the best thing he had seen in months. The robe here refers to the upper garment of the upper classes. The son was thus treated as a guest of honor. This points to another outstanding contrast. His shabby clothes would be covered by the best robe to honor him. This is a beautiful picture of being clothed in the righteousness of Christ. Next, he was given a ring. This spoke of authority. If a man gave his signet ring to another, it was the same as giving him power of attorney. To the Romans the ring was a sign of honor and nobility and those who wore a ring were distinguished from the common people. Finally, he was given sandals. Sandals were for children and not slaves and were a sign of freedom. In the dark days of our country's history, when we had slavery, the Negro spiritual expressed their dream of when all God's children got shoes, which spoke of their dream of freedom.[23] And we see that the slaves put each of these articles on the son, which would be a sign that he was also accepted as their master.

Then verses 23-24 speak of the party and celebration that occurred. The key here is to realize that the father was focusing on the son. He never once mentioned the son's sin, his disrespect, or his ingratitude. Why? He had been forgiven. That is grace. Abraham Lincoln was asked how he was going to treat the rebellious Southerners. His response, "I will treat them as if they had never been away."[24] It is important to notice why the celebration. Verse 24 gives the answer. His son was dead and had come to life. In other words, he had experienced a resurrection. This is a picture of salvation as expressed in Ephesians 2:4-6. He also had been lost, but was found. Who found him? The father at the edge of the village as he ran to him to bring about reconciliation. So, the celebration is a result of the resurrection and the son being found.

Now, we've seen that this parable further emphasizes God receiving sinners unto salvation. Once a person is saved, however, we need to never forget that our Father remains gracious and compassionate.

Yes, there are times when a true Christian can go off to the far country and wallow around in the pig pen. No, if he is a true Christian, I don't believe he will stay there, but it is possible to go there and when he returns, he finds that his Father is gracious and compassionate. When God's children sin, He is not there to condemn them, but He pities them and longs to show compassion for them. As we saw from the previous chapter in Isaiah 30:18, "Therefore the LORD longs to be gracious to you, And therefore He waits on high to have compassion on you." And David wrote in Psalm 103:12-14, "As far as the east is from the west, So far has He removed our transgressions from us. Just as a father has compassion on His children, So the LORD has compassion on those who fear Him. For He Himself knows our frame; He is mindful that we are but dust." There are three great truths to consider from this passage. First, we see that God's children are forgiven of their sins. We are in a state of forgiveness. Our sins are as far as the east is from the west. Stephen Charnock wrote, "When sin is pardoned, it is never charged again; the guilt of it can no more return than east can become west, or west becomes east."[25] Let me try to explain this further. If you were making a trip and headed due north or due south, eventually you would go in the opposite direction. In other words, north would become south and south would become north. If, however, you head east or west, you would never go in the opposite direction. East never becomes west and west never becomes east. Aren't you thankful that God didn't say that He had removed our transgressions as far as the north is from the south because that means there would have been a limit to His forgiveness. The second truth from this passage is that God's compassion is compared to that of a father. The word "compassion" is in the present tense which means that His compassion is always there for His children. It never fails. Charnock wrote, "No (child) is ever out of God's mind and therefore never out of His compassionate care. His eye pierceth into their dungeons and pities their miseries."[26] Finally, our Father is compassionate because He knows our frame and is mindful that we are but dust. Remember, when a child of God sins, our Father is not angry with us, but pities us.

Thomas Adams wrote, "So the Lord doth pity us, remembering our frame, considering that we are but dust; that our soul works by a lame instrument; and therefore he requires not that of an elemental composition, which He doth of angelic spirits....temptation assaults us, lusts buffet us, secular business diverts us, manifold is our weakness, but not beyond the Father's forgiveness."[27] Please understand, I'm not saying that we don't need to worry about sin as God's child because such is not true. Sin has serious consequences. As we learned in chapter 5, our loving Father disciplines His children. The point is this. When a child of God sins and comes to the Father, the Father longs to extend compassion. Why? He loves us. He yearns for us. As God said in Jeremiah 31:20, "Is Ephraim My dear son? Is he a delightful child? Indeed, as often as I have spoken against him, I certainly still remember him; Therefore My heart yearns for him; I will surely have mercy on him."

How Christian parents need to learn and apply this principle with our children. Just as we, parents, have sinned and failed when we were younger (and still do), we can expect that our children will sin and fail also. Some of their sins may be considered minor and some may be considered more serious and grave such as the prodigal son. The question is, however, how will we react toward them and treat them? Paul writes to the churches of Galatia, "Brethren, even if a man is caught in any trespass, you who are spiritual, restore such a one in a spirit of gentleness," (Galatians 6:1). John MacArthur wrote of a pastor who stated, "I have often thought that if I ever fall into a trespass, I will pray that I don't fall into the hands of those censorious, critical judges in the church. Let me fall into the hands of barkeepers, streetwalkers or dope peddlers, because such church people would tear me apart with their wagging, gossipy tongues, cutting me to shreds."[28] What was the pastor saying? He didn't expect to receive grace from the church family. I'm afraid that many of our children may not expect to receive grace from their parents when they have done something wrong or fallen into a sin. And if they don't receive grace and compassion in the less serious falls, we can surely expect that they won't come to us if they fall into sins which are more serious. As stated in chapter 3, a larger percentage of Christian teenage girls that get pregnant out of wedlock get abortions than non-Christian girls. Could it be that they don't expect to have grace and compassion demonstrated to them by their parents? As also stated in that chapter, one thing that may prevent parents from demonstrating grace and compassion to their children is pride in that the parents are more concerned about how they are perceived by their friends than their concern for their children.

Let me share with you a few examples of what I mean. One involved a pastor of a large church in a major city in our country. A father from another city called him requesting they search for his son whom he believed was in the city where this pastor lived and probably was involved in sinful and dangerous activities. Amazingly, the church found this young man and worked with him and finally, the young man had the courage to talk to his dad on the phone. So, he was in the pastor's office and the pastor called the young man's dad and told the dad that his son was in the office. Do you know what the first words from the dad were to his son? They were not, "I love you," or "I've missed you,'" or "Are you OK?" but, "Have you had a haircut yet?" The pastor stated the son ran out of his office and they never saw him again. Unlike the father in the parable, that father demonstrated no grace or compassion to his son and thus, more than likely, may never see his son again in this life.

A second example involved a teenage boy who was ministering in a children's ministry in a local church. An older lady who also ministered in this area always noticed that he was extremely careful to do exactly what he was told. It was as if he was even afraid to joke around with the other workers and have some fun. One day she commended him for the way he acted and his response was, "You don't cross my dad." The lady surmised that this teenager felt if he messed up the least little bit, he would not expect to receive grace and compassion from his dad.

A final example concerned a young man who would often go to bars and get drunk. Each time he got drunk, his father would go down and get him to bring him home to sleep it off. On one particular occasion, however, when the son got home he became abusive to his parents, especially his mother. The father demanded that the son leave and he told his son that he would never see him again. So, the son left and came back a couple of days later wanting to apologize to his parents. The father refused to see him and when the son made other efforts to see his father in the days to come, the father continued to refuse to see his son. Eventually the son left town and of course, had no contact with his father for years. One day, the son received word from someone in the town where his father lived, that his father was near death and he should come home and try again to talk with his father. Thus, the son went back to his hometown and when he got to the house, he asked the person who answered the door if he could see his dying father. The person went to the father to see if he wanted to see his son. The person came back and told the son that his father's reply was that he had said years ago that he would never see his son again and he meant it. That father demonstrated no grace and compassion for his son. Aren't you thankful, Christian, that our heavenly Father doesn't treat us like that for David wrote in Psalm 27:10, "For (If) my father or mother forsake me, But (Then) the LORD will take me up."

Now, the immediate question may be, how does grace and compassion fit in with disciplining our children? It fits quite well for they should go together. Please understand, to show our children grace and compassion does not mean that we won't discipline them, but with our discipline we will do it with grace and compassion. David knew this from personal experience with his heavenly Father. After being confronted by Nathan for his sin of adultery with Bathsheba and the murder of Uriah, David wrote in Psalm 51:1, "Be gracious to me, O God, according to Thy lovingkindness; According to the greatness of Thy compassion blot out my transgressions." Yes, David was disciplined severely but he still saw and experienced God's grace and compassion. Then in 1 Chronicles 21, we read of Satan standing up against Israel and moving David to number Israel. This act by David was evil in the sight of God. First Chronicles 21:8 states, "And David said to God, 'I have sinned greatly, in that I have done this thing. But now, please take away the iniquity of Thy servant, for I have done very foolishly." God sends Gad, David's seer, to give the option to choose one of three things for his discipline. In 1 Chronicles 21:11-12, Gad came to David with the following message. "Thus says the LORD, 'Take for yourself either three years of famine, or three months to be swept away before your foes, while the sword of your enemies overtakes you, or else three days of the sword of the LORD, even pestilence in the land, and the angel of the LORD destroying throughout all the territory of Israel.' Now, therefore, consider what answer I shall return to Him who sent me." Do you know what David chose? Verse 13 gives the answer. "And David said to Gad, 'I am in great distress; please let me fall into the hand of the LORD, for His mercies are very great. But do not let me fall into the hand of man.'" Did you notice that David had rather fall into the hands of almighty, omnipotent God rather than into the hands of man? Isn't that strange especially when we consider that Hebrews 10:31 says, "It is a terrifying thing to fall into the hands of the living God." We must realize, though, that Hebrews 10:31 refers to the wicked experiencing the wrathful hands of the living God while David knew God as his loving, heavenly Father whose hands are gracious and compassionate.

Earlier we looked at Psalm 103:13 which states that the LORD has compassion on those who fear Him, His children, just as a father has compassion on his children. And truly, we saw that demonstrated in the "Parable of the Gracious and Compassionate Father." We've also seen, though, that not all fathers or mothers demonstrate grace and compassion to their children. In that light, I want to share another example of grace and compassion being demonstrated to one who had fallen seriously whereby we, as parents, have another example to consider and imitate. It is the grace and compassion that Jesus demonstrated to Peter after his denials.

In Luke 22:31-32, Jesus told Peter that Satan had demanded to sift him like wheat, but Jesus had prayed for him. Peter then made the great boast that he would go to prison with Jesus and even die for Him. Jesus, however, told Peter that before the cock crowed, he would deny Jesus three times. Well, we all know what happened. Peter did deny Jesus three times. He even did so with curses. Yet, Jesus showed him such grace and compassion. And that grace and compassion began the moment the cock crowed. In Luke 22:61-62 we read, "And the Lord turned and looked at Peter. And Peter remembered the word of the Lord, how He had told him, 'Before a cock crows today, you will deny Me three times.' And he went out and wept bitterly." I don't believe that Jesus looked at Peter with anger, but with grace, love, compassion and pity and this broke Peter's heart. Let's never forget. As we saw earlier from Psalm 103:13-14, when a child of God sins, our Father doesn't look at us with anger, but with pity.

I'm sure that most of us have heard how Christians are viewed today toward those who are wounded. We are the only ones who shoot our wounded. This has made me reflect on Peter's denials. It was fortunate for Peter that he denied Jesus rather than most Christians today, for I'm afraid that most Christians today would have stoned Peter, but Jesus demonstrated grace and compassion. John Wesley was once traveling with General James Oglethorpe. Oglethorpe was angry with one of his subordinates. The man came to the general and humbly asked for his forgiveness. The general gruffly stated, "I never forgive." Wesley told the general, "Then I hope sir, that you never sin." That is how Christians are many times with grace. I once heard a mature Christian state that he had told someone, "If you let me down in a particular way, I will be the first one to cast stones at you." How sad. Where is the grace and compassion in such a statement? That is a statement that should be made only by one who has every right to cast a stone. In other words, a person who needs no grace. Jesus. And yet, we never hear of Him making such a statement or doing such a thing. Who were those who were always ready to cast stones? The Pharisees. And what was one of Jesus' problems with them? They were ungracious. Christopher Love wrote, "Many Christians are like a herd of deer. When one deer of the herd is wounded by the forester, all the rest leave and forsake him; they put him away from them and let the wounded deer shift for himself alone. There are many such uncompassionate souls who, if a man is in trouble of mind and has the arrows of God's wrath sticking in his soul, run away from him and leave him. Many men are thus lacking in tenderness and compassion towards tempted and troubled souls, but are full of censures, contempt, and rough dealing."[29] Think about this. Jesus, who was never a recipient of grace because He was full of grace, demonstrated grace and compassion to Peter. It all began with His look after Peter's denials, but it didn't end there.

On Resurrection Sunday, when the women went to the tomb, they found it empty, but also saw a young man wearing a white robe. Mark 16:6-7 states, "And he said to them, 'Do not be amazed; you are looking for Jesus the Nazarene, who has been crucified. He has risen; He is not here; behold, here is the place where they laid him. But go, tell His disciples and Peter, He is going before you into Galilee; there you will see Him, just as He said to you.'" Wasn't Peter a disciple? Why didn't he just say, "go tell His disciples" and that would have included Peter. Can you imagine how Peter felt throughout that weekend as a result of his denials? I'm sure he was devastated. Yet, by singling out Peter, grace and compassion was being shown to him.

Then in Luke 24 we read of Jesus appearing to the two men on the road to Emmaus. After their eyes were opened and they realized who Jesus was, they ran back to the disciples. Verse 34 records that they said, "The Lord has really risen, and has appeared to Simon."

Finally, in John 21 we read of Peter initiating a fishing trip with some of the other disciples. Have you ever thought why he did that? I have a speculation as to why he went fishing. Luke 5 records Jesus getting into Peter's boat after Peter had fished all night and caught nothing. Jesus taught from the boat and then had Peter go out to the deep water and let down his nets for a catch. Peter was hesitant for they had caught nothing all night, but he obeyed. They then caught so many fish that their nets began to break. And Peter fell down at Jesus' feet and said, "Depart from me, for I am a sinful man, O Lord!" (v.8). But Jesus told Peter, "Do not fear, from now on you will be catching men" (v.10).

Demonstrating Grace and Compassion to Your Children

Well, in John 21, I believe that Peter felt like such a failure that he could never be used by the Lord to catch men, so he would go back to something he could do, catch fish. Yet, the same thing happened as in Luke 5. They caught nothing until Jesus told them to cast their nets on the other side of the boat. They then caught so many fish that they were unable to haul them in. Peter jumped out of the boat to come to Jesus. Jesus proceeded to restore Peter to ministry by telling him that he could demonstrate his love for Jesus by tending and shepherding His lambs and sheep.

Have you noticed all that Jesus did to demonstrate grace and compassion to Peter? Then, on Pentecost, less than eight weeks after his denials, Peter preached that great sermon in which about three thousand souls were saved. I would like for you to consider the following question. If you had to choose someone to preach at Pentecost, whom would you have chosen? Would you have chosen someone whose last entry on his resume was the following? I arrogantly stated that I would die for Jesus; I then denied Jesus three times by lying that I even knew Him and even to the point of cursing and swearing. In other words, most of us would not have chosen Peter to preach at Pentecost. Yet, Jesus did. That is grace and compassion being demonstrated.

From Jesus' restoration of Peter there is one more vital truth for parents to learn and reflect on. We don't know all that Jesus spoke with Peter about during this process, but we can be sure that He spoke to him truth. My friend, Dr. Don Kistler, whom I quoted previously, once gave a sermon concerning the phrase "grace and truth." He mentioned that whenever grace, mercy or lovingkindness are paired with truth in the Bible, grace, mercy or lovingkindness are mentioned first and truth second. He pointed out that the order is significant. In other words, God is as concerned with the right disposition or demeanor as He is the right doctrine. He stated that "The truth of Christ without the heart of Christ is not the truth of Christ at all." If the truth is not delivered graciously or mercifully, then others likely will not hear the truth. In Ephesians 4:29, Paul wrote, "Let no unwholesome word proceed from your mouth, but only such a word as is good for edification according to the need of the moment, that it may give grace to those who hear it." From that verse we learn that any spoken word is unwholesome that does not give the necessary edification and grace to the hearer. We are not to be the reason others cannot hear the message. Yes, the message may offend, but the messenger is not to offend. And many times, sin may have to be confronted or exposed. Proverbs 16:6a tells us, though, "By lovingkindness and truth iniquity is atoned for." Consequently, grace or mercy is to make way for the truth to be accepted.

How does this apply to Christian parents? How often, when our children fall into some sin, especially the more serious sins, do we, as parents, beat them over the head with the truth from God's word rather than presenting it to them with grace or mercy? We often get upset at our children, especially our teenagers, for not hearing us. Could it be that they don't hear us because we are not talking to them with grace and mercy? Unfortunately, there have been times when I've used God's word to beat other Christians and my sons rather than presenting it with grace and mercy. It is my prayer that I would always declare our Father's glorious truth with whomever, but especially my sons, with grace and mercy.

As I close this chapter, I want to ask us parents a very important question. If one of your children went off into the far country in rebellion like the prodigal did or failed you like Peter did Jesus, how would you respond to them? Would you seek to demonstrate grace and compassion to them like our heavenly Father and Jesus did or would you be more like the three examples displayed by the earthly fathers previously mentioned? Oh, may we be found faithful to be parents that demonstrate grace and compassion to our children. After all, if you are a child of God, your heavenly Father has demonstrated grace and compassion to you over and over again.

Chapter Eight

Being an Encourager to Your Children

> Thus Sarah obeyed Abraham, calling
> him lord, and you have become her
> children if you do what is right without
> being frightened by any fear.
> —1 Peter 3:6

> "Now it was in the heart of my father
> David to build a house for the name
> of the LORD, the God of Israel.
> But the LORD said to my father
> David, 'Because it was in your
> heart to build a house for My name,
> you did well that it was in your heart.'"
> —1 Kings 8:17-18

One of my favorite saints in the New Testament is Barnabas. Probably most of us don't know what his real name was because it is only used once in the New Testament. As Acts 4:36 tells us, his real name was Joseph and he was a Levite of Cyprian birth. That verse also informs us, however, that he was called Barnabas, by the apostles which means "Son of Encouragement." Names in the Bible often depicted the character of the particular person(s).

In fact, what the disciples did by renaming Joseph, Barnabas, was also done by Jesus with some of His disciples. Mark 3 records Jesus choosing the twelve. Mark tells us that to Simon Jesus gave the name "Peter" and to James and John, the sons of Zebedee, He gave the name "Boanerges", which means "Sons of Thunder" (Mark 3:16-17). Now truly, "Sons of Thunder" was an appropriate name for James and John. In Luke 9:51-55, we read that the days were approaching for Jesus' ascension and thus, He resolutely was setting His face to go to Jerusalem. He sent messengers ahead to a village in Samaria to make arrangements for his arrival. This village, however, did not receive Jesus because He was journeying with His face toward Jerusalem. This led James and John to say to Jesus, "Lord, do You want us to command fire to come down from heaven and consume them?" They were acting like their names, "Sons of Thunder."

Well, Barnabas, "Son of Encouragement," certainly lived up to his name. No. He was not perfect for as Galatians 2 tells us, Barnabas was carried away by the hypocrisy of Peter and other Jews when they withdrew from eating with the Gentiles because they feared the party of the circumcision who had come from James. Still, however, the pattern of Barnabas' life, as depicted in Scripture, was one of an encourager in the lives of those he ministered to. Let me give just a couple of examples of Barnabas' encouragement. Acts 9 records Paul's dramatic conversion on the road to Damascus. While in Damascus Paul proclaimed Jesus as the Son of God in the synagogues (v. 20). The Jews were amazed and confounded at the change in Paul (v. 21-22). Because he was now seen as a threat, the Jews plotted to kill Paul, but he learned of their plot and escaped as fellow believers lowered him in a large basket through an opening in the wall. Paul goes to Jerusalem and seeks to associate with the disciples but they were afraid of him and not convinced of the reality of his conversion (v. 26). It was Barnabas, however, that took Paul to the apostles whereby he could share with them about his experience with the Lord (v. 27). I can imagine how this encouraged Paul that Barnabas did this for him.

One of the greatest examples of Barnabas living up to his name involved his cousin, Mark. The church at Antioch sent Paul and Barnabas out on a missionary journey, their first one. They took Mark along with them. While on the journey, however, Mark leaves them and returns to Jerusalem. Paul and Barnabas continue on with the missionary journey. Later on, Acts 15:36-41 records Paul telling Barnabas that he wanted them to go on another missionary journey and visit the brethren in those cities where they had proclaimed God's word previously to see how they were doing. Barnabas wanted to take Mark along again, but Paul refused because Mark had deserted them on their first journey. The disagreement between Paul and Barnabas was so severe that they separated from one another. Barnabas took Mark and they sailed to Cyprus. Paul chose Silas and they traveled through Syria and Cilicia, strengthening the churches. Nothing more is said about Barnabas in the book of Acts. Well, how do we know that he was an encourager to Mark? If we go to 2 Timothy, referred to earlier as Paul's death bed letter, 2 Timothy 4:11 records Paul writing to Timothy, "Pick up Mark and bring him with you, for he is useful to me for service." Why the drastic change in Paul's attitude toward Mark between his disagreement with Barnabas prior to the second missionary journey and what he writes as he is facing death? I believe the difference is a result of Barnabas being an encourager to Mark. Parents, what Barnabas was to Mark, we are to be to our children.

Even though Barnabas was an encourager to others, the Scripture says very little about how he did it. The Scripture, however, gives some great examples of how our loving, heavenly Father encourages His children that parents can learn from and seek to imitate. I want to focus on the two passages of Scripture that introduced this chapter. At first glance, it may appear that they have very little to do with God, our Father, being an encourager to His children, but when we examine them in light of the context, hopefully this great truth will become evident.

The first passage of Scripture is found in 1 Peter 3. First Peter 3 starts out by instructing wives to be submissive to their husbands, even if they are disobedient to the word. In other words, unbelieving husbands. What is the purpose for wives being submissive, even to unbelieving husbands? So that their husbands may be won to the Lord without a word as they observe the chaste and respectful behavior of their wives (v.1-2). Consequently, wives are not just to be concerned about their external adornment, but rather they are to be concerned about the hidden person of the heart, characterized by a gentle and quiet spirit that is precious in God's eyes (v.3-4). Those qualities were the way holy women in former times adorned themselves as they were submissive to their husbands (v.5). From our key verse then, verse 6, the example of such a submissive wife was Sarah in that she obeyed Abraham, calling him "lord."

It is important for us to recall the incident that Peter writes of concerning Sarah and Abraham. In Genesis 18, the LORD and two angels appeared to Abraham by the oaks of Mamre. Abraham immediately made preparations to serve his three special guests a meal. After the meal, Abraham was told that this time next year the LORD would return to him and Sarah would have the child that had been promised many years earlier. Genesis 18:11 emphasizes that both Abraham and Sarah were old and that Sarah was past childbearing. We're also told that Sarah was listening from the tent door (v.10). What was her response? "Praise the Lord, I'm finally going to be a mother!" Not quite. Genesis 18:12 gives the answer. "And Sarah laughed to herself, saying, 'After I have become old, shall I have pleasure, my lord being old also?'" The LORD asks Abraham why Sarah had laughed and concerning her unbelief He then asks, "Is anything too difficult for the LORD?"(v.13-14). Sarah denied that she laughed, but the LORD told her that He knew she had laughed (v.15).

Did you notice all that Sarah did wrong from this incident? She laughed at a promise made by the LORD. She lied to the LORD in saying that she had not laughed. And yes, she called Abraham "lord" but that was in the context of a statement of unbelief. Yet, in 1 Peter 3:6, none of what Sarah did wrong (her sin) was mentioned, but what she did right, her submissiveness to Abraham in calling him "lord." Jeremiah Burroughs wrote, "Whatever you do, though there are never so many imperfections in it, if God can spy out the least good thing in you, He will take notice of that and cast away all evil. If God sees anything of His own Spirit in you He will be sure to take notice of that. If there is just one dust of gold, though it is mixed with an abundance of dross, God will not lose it but will find it. God is not so strict to mark what is done amiss by His children, but He is strict to mark what is done well by them."[1] That is grace. That is a loving Father being an encourager to His children.

Let me share with you another example of this principle. On several occasions I have played a word association game with other Christians, to include tribal pastors in India. I told them that I would mention the name of a Biblical character and then I wanted them to share the first thought that came to their mind. The Biblical character I mentioned was Lot. Invariably, the first thing that came to their minds was something negative about him as recorded in Genesis. Only a very few times has a person given the answer I was looking for as found in 2 Peter 3:7. Lot is referred to as righteous. Probably most of us don't associate Lot with righteousness, but a lot (no pun intended) of the sin that was displayed in his life. When we think of Lot, our natural tendency is to remember his selfishness by taking the best land when he separated from Abraham. We may think of his moving to Sodom or his offering his two daughters to the wicked men of Sodom rather than giving them the two angels they requested to have illicit relations with. There was also the incident of his drunkenness, which resulted in him fathering a child by both of his daughters. So, there is so much that we could associate Lot with that is not righteous. His heavenly Father, however, pulls out the gold of righteousness and mentions that in 2 Peter 3 and none of the dross. In fact, if you examine the failures of the saints in the Old Testament, when they are referred to in the New Testament, their failures are never mentioned. Only what they did right. That is true even of Rahab, the harlot. Rahab is mentioned twice in the New Testament, in Hebrews 11 as a woman of faith and in James 2 as one who demonstrated that her faith was genuine by her works. Yes, she is referred to as "the harlot" in those two passages but that is only for the purpose of identification, so that we would not confuse her with a different woman that may have been named Rahab. Her heavenly Father emphasized her great faith. Here again, such are examples of a loving Father being an encourager to His children. And I pray Christian, that this great truth is an encouragement to you from your Father.

At this point, I want to share a word picture, which further illustrates this great truth. I will share this word picture from a negative view point and then, from the proper positive view point. There was a concert pianist who gave a performance and after he had finished, he received a standing ovation from the audience. He went back stage and someone encouraged him to go back out and further acknowledge the audience's approval. He was reluctant to do so and when asked why, he pointed to the balcony and one person who was seated, rather than standing and applauding. He stated that person was his teacher and if his teacher wasn't pleased, it mattered little to him what the rest of the audience thought. So many pastors, myself included, have used that word picture, to make Christians feel guilty in that if their heavenly Father isn't pleased with us in whatever we may do, it matters little what others think. Granted, a Christian's desire should be to please our heavenly Father regardless of what anyone else thinks, but this word picture almost portrays our heavenly Father as if He is not pleased unless we are perfect in what we seek to do for His glory. Based on Burroughs statement and the examples we saw from Scripture, the positive viewpoint of that word picture is that, as I've heard Steve Brown say, our Father would be standing and applauding for His child, even if no one else was. That is grace and how encouraging that ought to be to Christians.

The second passage of Scripture which demonstrates our Father being an encourager to His children is found in 1 Kings 8:17-18. The context of this chapter is the ark of the covenant being brought into the finished temple and the dedication of the temple. The verses that concern us, though, are taken from Solomon's address to the people. He stated that the heart of his father, David, was to build a house for God. David's heart and plan to build this house for God are found in 2 Samuel 7. God, through the prophet Nathan, however, told David that he would not be allowed to build the temple, but that his son would. Solomon states, though, that the LORD had told his father that because it was in his heart to build a house for His name, he did well. Burroughs wrote, "Suppose you cannot do anything. If there is even a will, a desire in you, God accepts the will for the deed."[2] This is another example of our loving Father being an encourager to His children.

Several years ago I met a dear couple who was preparing to go to the mission field in Ivory Coast, Africa. God had given them a real heart for the people of the Ivory Coast. After all the training and necessary preparations, they eventually made it to the Ivory Coast. Not long after they were there the wife became pregnant with twins. There were some complications during the pregnancy which resulted in the family having to return to the States until the birth of the twins. After the twins were born, however, one of them had some medical problems which delayed their return to the Ivory Coast. Eventually, it seemed as if the young twin was well enough for the entire family to return to the mission field. The twin, though, developed more medical complications which resulted in the family having to return to the states again because they could not get the proper medical care in Africa. Finally, they realized that they could not return to the Ivory Coast at all because of their child's health. They were heartbroken because they had such a love for the people of the Ivory Coast. They couldn't understand why God had closed the door to this ministry which He had laid upon their hearts earlier. One day I was talking to the dad and he was expressing his disappointment over the fact that they couldn't return to this particular mission field. I shared with him the passage from 1 Kings 8 reference David's desire and then Burroughs' observation. I told him that his Father saw his heart and desire and accepted his family's desire to go back to the Ivory Coast as if they actually had gone back. This encouragement from his heavenly Father brought real comfort to him. Aren't you thankful, child of God, that you have a Father who is such an encourager to you?

Oh, parents, how we need to be an encourager to our children. The author of Hebrews wrote in Hebrews 10:25 that we are to encourage one another. That is in the context of believers seeking to stimulate one another to love and good deeds by not forsaking our own assembling together. Well, if we are to do that within the family of God, how much more should we do that within our own families to our children.

I once read a devotional entitled, "Booster Words," by Dave Branon. He spoke of the benefit of booster shots for our physical health to protect us from dangerous diseases and compared them to "booster words" which we should give to others to encourage them.[3] As I seek to make application of this principle for parents to be an encourager to their children, I really want to focus on booster actions and words. I think the best way to do this is to give practical examples of those who were encouragers to their children and those who weren't. Most of these are real life examples. There is only one example, a movie, that is fictional but hopefully it will illustrate this principle.

When we looked at our heavenly Father being an encourager to His children, we saw that if He sees the least little bit of gold in our actions, even though it is full of dross, He focuses on the gold. What a difference that would make in our children's lives if parents did the same for them. When our children are very young, usually parents are pretty good about this. If our children paint us a picture or make us a card for a special occasion, we usually say how much we like it and how pretty it is, even if there are numerous mistakes. And in most cases we put it on the refrigerator for everyone to see. How that quickly changes, though, within just a few years. A prime example of this is what I've seen in Little League Baseball. Sadly, I've witnessed parents get so frustrated with their children for making the same mistakes that major leaguers who get paid millions of dollars a year make. Rather than encouraging their children, parents often condemn and tear their children down when they don't play like the parent wants them to. I've often wondered if many parents don't try to live unfulfilled dreams of their own through their children and thus, put undue pressure on them rather than being an encourager to them in whatever the children do.

What should the parents do? Thomas Adams wrote, "The father gives his son a bow and arrows, bids him shoot to such a mark: he draws his utmost strength, lets go cheerfully: the arrow drops far short, yet the son is praised, the father pleased."[4] A beautiful illustration of this is found in the movie, "The Music Man." If you ever saw that movie, you probably remember that Robert Preston played Professor Harold Hill. Professor Hill was really a con man who came to River City, Iowa, and stated there was trouble there which begins with "T" and rhymes with "P" which stands for pool. So, he wanted to clean this trouble up by starting a band. In reality, however, he wanted to sell the city on a band and once he had collected money from them, he would leave town. Of course, Harold Hill was no music professor. He had no music training whatsoever whereby he could teach others. Eventually, he was exposed for who he really was, which caused an uproar among the people. Parents had paid for band uniforms and instruments and there was nothing to show for it. As the town leaders brought Harold Hill before the town's people, they were ready to tar and feather him. All of a sudden the band members walked into the town meeting. Harold Hill was forced to lead them in a song and this would demonstrate that he was a phony. He was hesitant to do so because he knew they couldn't play. Sure enough, as he conducted the band they sounded awful. Missed notes, no rhythm and no harmony. Unexpectedly, however, a parent jumped up and shouted, "My Barney. That's my Barney playing the tuba." Then another parent jumped up and shouted, "That's my Eddie playing the clarinet." Still another parent shouted, "Davy. That's my Davy playing." What were these parents doing? They weren't focusing on all the missed notes and awful sounds, but focused on their children playing a band instrument and were seeking to encourage them.

Why is it so important that parents be an encourager to their children? It is because of the impressions it will make upon them and then the lasting effects. T. Dewitt Talmage relates an incident that illustrates this point. He was in a house in a Long Island village and saw a beautiful tree that had an unusual crook in it. He asked the owner how this had occurred. The owner stated that he had planted the tree and when it was a year old, he went to New York to work for a couple of years. When he came back, he was informed that someone had allowed something to stand against the tree and thus, the crook became permanent. Talmage then applied that to a parent's influence upon their children. When parents fail to encourage their children properly, it can have lasting effects. He stated that he knew why Lord Byron was bad. One day his mother saw him limping across the floor with his unsound foot and said, "Get out of my way, you lame brat!" Talmage's response was, "What chance for a boy like that!"[5]

In a previous chapter I mentioned a 3 ½ year old Muslim girl calling Jews "pigs." Sadly, I've heard of family members, who were Christians, calling young children within their own family similar type names and even worse. Yes, that young Muslim girl had been taught to refer to Jews in that way, but at 3 ½ she was just repeating what she had learned by continuous repetition. To call anybody such derogatory names is bad enough, but for Christian family members to do it to young children within their own family is reprehensible and could have lasting effects that are detrimental to their children.

Not only do our young children need for their parents to be encouragers to them, but parents need to continually do this for their children, regardless of their age. Let me share several examples to illustrate what I mean. I have a friend who told me about a young girl whose parents were in the ministry but she never received any type of encouragement from them as she grew up. So, music became an outlet for her to fill the void and hopefully to finally receive some encouragement from her parents. Still, however, whenever she performed, her parents never attended one of her performances. I mentioned previously that parents are to be encouragers through "booster" actions and words. These parents were obviously there to encourage those they ministered to with words and actions, but they failed to do it for their own daughter. I wonder what impression and influence this had on her as she grew older. I'm afraid to speculate.

Another example involves an incident that I witnessed first hand. There was a man that was getting ready to go out of the country for almost two weeks. Two of his teenage children brought him to catch his ride to the airport. As they were leaving, the very last words that he said to them were not, "I love you" or "I'll miss you" or "I'm thankful for you" but, "Make sure you repent every day." Yes, the Christian life is to be one of continual repentance and belief, but what were this dad's words saying to his children? "I know you are going to mess up." What did we see about our heavenly Father in the previous chapter? He is gracious and compassionate. We saw that from Luke 15 and Psalm 103:13, but I want to emphasize further Psalm 103:14. After verse 13 states that God had compassion on His children like a father for his children, verse 14 states, "For He Himself knows our frame; He is mindful that we are but dust." I've mentioned before my friend, Don Kistler. We were talking about that verse one day and he said something like, "What do we expect out of dust? Nothing. When I stamp my foot in a pile of dust, it doesn't float down nicely and form the words, 'Have a nice day, Kistler.' Rather, it gets my shoes dirty." Christian, aren't you thankful that our heavenly Father doesn't focus on our messing up so often, which we all do, but He is an encourager to us as we saw earlier in the chapter.

Then, parents need to be encouragers of their children even when the children are adults. One of my favorite preachers was Dr. Stephen Olford, a contemporary and friend of Billy Graham, who passed away a few years ago. In 1994, it was my privilege to attend a conference at Word of Life in Hudson, Florida with Dr. Olford and his son, David, as the guest speakers. The conference began on a Monday night and Dr. Olford was the first speaker. As usual, this gifted man's message was dynamic and anointed by God. The next morning David was scheduled to be the first speaker. When David got up to speak, he mentioned that several of the men had come up to him and told him that his dad was a hard act to follow. Then David told us that he didn't have to follow his dad. His dad had instilled in him throughout life that "God does not make duplicates. He only makes originals." He didn't have to be like his dad. He didn't have to be like anyone. Wouldn't it be great if parents treated their children like this? I mentioned in a previous chapter of statements that parents use such as, "Why can't you be like your brother or sister?" They can't be like them because they are an original and not a duplicate of their brother or sister. And if parents treated all their children like originals and thus, not compare them to others, I've got to believe this would be a great encouragement to the children. After David shared what his father had instilled in him, I thought to myself, "What an encouragement that must have been to David." And as David spoke, he was gifted and anointed by God in his own right. The point is this. Dr. Olford had been an encourager to his son to be what God had made him to be and not what others wanted him to be and even though David was a mature adult, his dad was continuing to encourage him in this way. And all throughout the conference, Dr. Olford would often refer to something that his son had shared or taught.

The contrast of Dr. Olford's actions is those parents who demean their grown children rather than encourage them. Sadly, I've seen this on many occasions. As stated in a previous chapter, parents are to instruct their children. And I believe this instruction should be as long as the parents live. Parents continue to be a valuable source of information for their children even when the children become adults because of the experiences and wisdom that the parents have obtained and continue to obtain over the years. And this wisdom and information can be used to encourage their children. Yet, so often parents say things in such demeaning ways that no encouragement or information is received. Only discouragement and heartache. Such parents only focus on the negative and find fault with their children rather than looking for the positive whereby they can encourage their children. And in many cases, what the parent gets so upset about involves the way a material possession is treated or the way something looks.

The example I'm about to share I received in an e-mail and it involves a five-year-old girl, but depicts the same attitude that was emphasized in the previous sentence. A mother punished her young daughter for wasting a roll of expensive gold wrapping paper. Money was tight and she got more upset when the child used the gold paper to decorate a box to put under the Christmas tree. On Christmas morning the little girl brought the wrapped box to her mother and said, "This is for you, Momma." The mother was then embarrassed in how she had over reacted toward her daughter, but she soon became angry again when she opened the box and saw that it was empty. In a harsh manner she said to her daughter, "Don't you know, young lady, when you give someone a present, there's supposed to be something inside the package?" With tears in her eyes she said to her mother, "Oh, Momma, it's not empty. I blew kisses into it until it was full." These words crushed the mother. She fell on her knees and then put her arms around her daughter and asked for her forgiveness for her anger. A short time later the young girl was killed in an accident. The mother kept that gold box by her bed the rest of her life. Whenever she faced discouraging times or problems, she would open the box and take out an imaginary kiss and remember the love of her young daughter who had put it there. What did the mother's attitude depict initially? She got so angry over what she saw as a misuse or waste of a possession, gold wrapping paper. Fortunately, she soon realized what was truly important. Here again, I'm aware of numerous examples where parents have gotten angry with their own grown children in a similar fashion over some possession, and I'm not talking about an expensive possession. What does such an attitude say? The grown child has to perform or act in a particular way or the parent gets upset. In such a case, the parent demonstrates that they are not really concerned about the relationship, but only about themselves.

Such depicts a selfish and critical spirit. This will be discussed more in the next chapter, but the bottom line is that the relationship is based on performance and not unconditional love.

I would like to close this chapter with one more example that will hopefully summarize this vital principle. I also received it as an e-mail from a friend. It was entitled, "That's My Child." The person who authored this story (author unknown) stated that he was watching some children, about five or six years old, playing soccer. He didn't know any of the children, so he could enjoy the game without being anxious over who won or lost. Initially, the two teams were evenly matched. Neither team scored in the first period. It was fun watching these young children because they fell over their own feet, stumbled over the ball and often when they kicked at the ball, they missed it. It didn't seem to matter, however, for they were having fun.

In the second period, the Team One coach pulled out his first team and put in the less talented children, except for his best player who guarded the goal. Then the game took a dramatic turn as the Team Two coach left his best players in. Obviously, winning was the most important thing to this coach even though the children were only five or six. Of course, Team One was now no match for Team Two. Team Two swarmed around the Team One goalie. He was a great athlete for his age, but he could not compete when there were three or four children from the other team who were also very good. So, Team Two began to score. Team One's goalie gave it everything he could by throwing his body in front of incoming balls and trying to stop them. Team Two quickly scored two goals and this really upset the goalie of Team One. He was doing everything he could possibly do to help his team. Shouting, running and diving to try and prevent any further goals. He covered a boy who had the ball, but that boy quickly kicked it to another boy twenty feet away and by the time the goalie got repositioned, it was too late and Team Two had scored a third goal.

Soon the observer learned who the goalie's parents were. They were neat looking people and it was apparent that the dad had just come from his office for he was still dressed in a suit and tie. Both parents yelled encouragement to their son. The observer became absorbed watching the boy on the field and his parents on the sidelines.

After the third goal, the little boy changed. He realized that he couldn't stop the other team. He didn't quit, but he became desperate. The father also changed at this point. He had begun the second period by urging his son to try harder and offering advice and encouragement. But now, the father became anxious and began to grieve for the pain that his son was feeling.

Team Two then scored a fourth goal. The goalie needed help, but there was no help to be found. After retrieving the ball from the net and giving it to the referee, he began to cry. Huge tears rolled down his cheeks. He then went to his knees, put his fists to his eyes and cried more tears of helplessness and broken-heartedness. After this young boy went to his knees, the observer saw the father start on the field. His wife clutched his arm and said, "Jim, don't. You'll embarrass him." The father, however, broke loose from her grip and ran onto the field even though he wasn't supposed to since the game was still in progress. The father picked up his son so that everyone would know that was his boy and held him close and cried with him. He then carried his son off the field and when he got close to the sidelines, he was heard to say, "Scotty. I'm so proud of you. You were great out there. I want everyone to know that you are my son." Through tears Scotty responded, "Daddy, I couldn't stop them. I tried, Daddy. I tried and tried, and they scored on me." The father then said, "Scotty, it doesn't matter how many times they scored on you. You're my son, and I'm proud of you. I want you to go back out there and finish the game. I know you want to quit, but you can't. And son, you're going to get scored on again, but it doesn't matter. Go on now."

The observer noticed that there was a difference in this little boy. He ran back on the field and the other team scored two more times, but it was OK. Why? The father's encouragement that even though the son was getting scored on and he couldn't stop them, it meant so much to know that his father was still proud of him. Isn't this father's encouragement a contrast with the father who told his children to make sure they repented everyday or the parents who demean their children and even call them derogatory names?

The observer then put what he had seen on the spiritual level as it related to his relationship with his heavenly Father. He stated that he gets scored on every day even though he tries so hard. He often recklessly would throw his body in every direction as he struggled with temptation and sin. Yet, Satan laughs as he scores again. So, the tears come and he goes to his knees, sinful, convicted and helpless. Then, his heavenly Father rushes onto the field in front of the whole world with its jeering and laughing and picks him up, hugs him and says, "Child, I'm so proud of you. You were great out there. I want everyone to know that you are My child, and because I control the outcome of this game, I declare you The Winner." Christian, aren't you thankful that your heavenly Father is an encourager to you, His child, rather than one who always focuses on your failures and thus, is quick to condemn you? The Bible says that we are to encourage one another day by day. Parents, how vital it is that the primary focus of our encouragement be to our children regardless of their age.

Chapter Nine

Loving Your Children Unconditionally

> For the LORD has comforted His people,
> And will have compassion on His afflicted.
> But Zion said, "The LORD has forsaken me,
> And the LORD has forgotten me."
> "Can a woman forget her nursing child,
> And have no compassion on the son of her womb?
> Even these may forget, but I will not forget you.
> Behold, I have inscribed you on the palms
> of My hands."
> —Isaiah 49:13c-16a

A pastor announced to his congregation that the next Sunday he was going to preach a one-word sermon. Everyone waited in anticipation of what his one-word sermon would be. So, when the next Sunday came, as it was time for him to get up and preach, he came to the pulpit and said, "Love" and then sat down. Of course, I would never recommend that a pastor preach a one-word sermon because it is his responsibility to faithfully feed the flock that God has entrusted to him. Still, however, love is a very powerful word when used in the proper context. Let me illustrate. Unfortunately, in the English language *love* is used in many different ways. I love God. I love my family. I love my work. I love my pet. I love sports. I love ice cream. I love my car. Hopefully, our love for God and family is much different than our love for such things as work, sports and cars, although there are many who love their work, sports, cars and such other things more than God and family. The point I'm trying to make is this. In the English language, when a person uses the word "love" it is hard to tell the degree and commitment of such love. That is why the Greek language is helpful. In the Greek there are several words that are translated into English as love, but the use of these Greek words emphasizes the difference between them. For example, the Greek word "eros" from which we get our English word "erotic" refers to a romantic love. This Greek word is never used in the New Testament. Then there is the word "storge" which refers to a natural affection or emotional type of love. This is a type of love that can come or go. The Greek word "phileo" speaks of a love of friendship or a brotherly love. Our U. S. city, Philadelphia, means "the city of brotherly love." The Greek word "agape", the highest type of love, refers to a love that is unconditional. Spiro Zodhiates defines the Greek verb "agapao" as "To esteem, love, indicating a direction of the will and finding one's joy in something or someone. It differs from "phileo," to love, indicating feelings, warm affection, the kind of love expressed by a kiss."[1] Agape describes the love that our heavenly Father has for His children.

In order to understand this, I want to examine three statements which describe one's love for another person. The three statements are: "I love you if," or "I love you because," or "I love you." Now, if most of us were asked which statement would describe our love for our family, friends or fellow Christians, I'm sure that we would say, "I love you." That is great because it depicts a love that is unconditional. Unfortunately, that unconditional love is not truly lived out, but rather a love that is depicted by one or both of the first two statements. What do the first two statements depict? A love that is conditional. Thus, if the condition is not met, then the love is not there. For example, the statement, "I love you if" depicts a love that is based on performance. If the person does not act or perform in a certain way, then the other person withholds his love in some way. This often occurs in friendships. Friends may say that their friendship is based on unconditional love, but if one friend does not communicate in the way or with the frequency that the other friend desires, then that friend actually withholds love in some way from the friend who did not perform in the way that was expected. I enjoy collecting and reading poems about friendship based on unconditional love. One of my favorite poems talks about someone being a "Special Person" to their friend. One of the lines in that poem states that even though the friends may be separated by time and distance, when they reunite, they continue on as if they had never been separated, because in reality, they weren't separated. What would keep them united even though these friends were physically separated? It is unconditional love, not based on performance.

The second conditional love statement, "I love you because" depicts a love that is based on certain conditions being met. If those conditions aren't met to the degree that the person giving the love desires, then he withholds that love. Let me give a couple of examples related to this conditional type of love. The first example involved a couple who were dating and the young lady stated that she loved the young man. I was told that when asked what she liked about him, she stated that she liked his looks, money, the car he drove and the way he dressed. The question arises, what if one or all of those things were taken away? Would she still have loved him?

The second example involved Dave Roever, a committed Christian, who served our country in the Viet Nam War with the Navy Seals. As he was getting ready to throw a white phosphorus hand grenade during a battle, he was hit by enemy fire and the grenade exploded. This resulted in his being burned badly and critically injured. I won't go into all the details, but it was a miracle that he survived. He was taken to a hospital in Japan. While there he asked for a mirror and when he looked at his face, he couldn't believe what he saw. He saw himself as a creature with half his skull showing and the other half of his face swollen. He was on morphine and this affected his thinking and in his words, "the mirror became a tool of the enemy." Satan basically told him that he needed to kill himself for he was a half-headed freak and his wife was a beautiful, teenage girl. So, Dave tried to kill himself, but in God's sovereign grace, Dave pulled out the wrong tube. Eventually, he was brought to a hospital in America. There were 13 young men in the same area as Dave and he was the only one who survived. In the bed next to him was a helicopter pilot who had been shot down. The helicopter exploded and he was burned over his entire body with third degree burns. There was no skin left on his body and nobody had ever survived such a burning. He lived long enough, however, to see his wife walk into this hospital room. When she saw her husband, she took off her wedding ring and threw it on the bed. She told her husband, "You're embarrassing. I couldn't walk down the street with you." She then walked out the door and left her husband to die. Thus, her love was really conditional and part of those conditions was how he obviously looked.

As Dave witnessed this event, he was fearful as to what his beautiful, teenage wife would say and do. Surely, she couldn't love him either. When she arrived, Dave watched her walk to his bed and was looking to see if her wedding rings were coming off. She picked up the chart on his bed and read the name, Dave Roever. She then turned his hand over to read his tag to make sure this was her husband because she could not recognize him as a result of all the injuries he had suffered. Dave's heart was sinking because he just knew that she would walk out also. A smile then broke across her face and she kissed his mutilated face. She looked at Dave and said, "I just want you to know I really love you. Welcome home Davy."[2] Her love was not based on the condition of how Dave looked. Whether his face was smooth or scarred, she just loved him.

Christian, aren't you thankful that your heavenly Father loves you unconditionally? It is not based on your performance or based on you meeting certain conditions. He just loves you unconditionally. As we saw in chapter 1 from Isaiah 43:4ab, our Father says to His children, "Since you are precious in My sight, since you are honored and I love you." He chose to love us unconditionally. There are so many verses in the Bible that speak of this love and from which volumes could be written. I once heard of a little boy, too young to read, flipping page after page in his Bible. His dad asked him what he was doing to which the boy responded, "I'm reading the Bible." The dad then asked him what it said. With each page the boy read, "God is love. God is love." Truly every page in the Bible could depict God's love for His children in some way. I have chosen one of my favorite passages from one of my favorite books in the Old Testament, Isaiah 49:13c-16a, to illustrate this great principle.

The context of Isaiah 49 emphasizes that there is a glorious future for both the "Servant of the LORD" and His people Israel, even though the present circumstances they were facing were not glorious, but rather were gloomy and full of misery.[3] If we, as God's children, are honest with ourselves, isn't that a struggle that we often face? Yes, we know of our glorious future in eternity, but the reality of life is that we often face circumstances that are difficult and many times seem devastating. And what is our response many times when experiencing such circumstances? Father, do you know what I'm going through? Are you still there? That is exactly what God's people did as recorded in Isaiah 49:14. In this verse, Zion does not refer to a city but God's people. You notice that verse starts out with a contrast word, "but." It is a contrast with what was previously stated in verse 13cd with what is stated in verse 14. It is a contrast between a promise from God for His people with what His people felt they were experiencing. The promise was that God has comforted His people and will have compassion on His afflicted. God's people, however, in the midst of difficult circumstances felt just the opposite. They felt that God had forsaken and forgotten them. When you think about it, for God's people, there could be nothing worse than what is stated in verse 14 if that were true. Thankfully, it is not true. Because of Jesus experiencing God's wrath on our behalf at the cross and thus, being forsaken by God (Matthew 27:46), we have the promise that He will never desert us or forsake us (Hebrews 13:5). And rather than forgetting us, we have His promise that He will remember our sins no more (Isaiah 43:25). Even with these great promises, however, at times our faith, like Israel's, may be weak and thus, we may feel forsaken and forgotten by God. Basically then, Israel was saying that God didn't love them anymore as shown by His forsaking and forgetting them. Have you ever felt that you were unloved by your heavenly Father in that it seemed as if He had forsaken and forgotten you through the difficult circumstances that you were facing? I'm sure that most of us would answer "yes" to that question if we were truly honest with ourselves.

In verse 15, though, God emphasizes the impossibility of what His people felt in verse 14 with an analogy comparing His love and thoughts for His children with that of a mother for her nursing child. He asks, "Can a woman forget her nursing child, And have no compassion on the son of her womb?" Of course, God asks this question expecting a "no" answer. It may be hard for men to really understand the significance of this statement. I know it was for me. Now, with what I'm about to write, you may think that my elevator doesn't go to the top floor. Well, that may be true, but when I was given the book, *The Womanly Art of Breastfeeding*, Isaiah 49:15 became much more meaningful to me. This book was not written as a spiritual book, but was written to encourage mothers to breast feed their children because of the medical benefit and the security it would provide for them. Still, though, as I read the book I learned a great deal about the intimacy and bond that God has established between a mother and her nursing child. We need to understand what God has given between a mother and her nursing baby is just a glimpse of the beautiful love relationship between the heavenly Father and His children. I would like to share some selected portions from this book, which depicts the truth stated in Isaiah 49:15ab.

> "Babies are to love. They are happiest when snuggled close to mother, nursing very often. They are meant to be within close proximity of her warm breast and the sound of her voice. The all-important mother-child bond replaces the umbilical cord. We cannot start too early in giving a child continuous, warm, consistent affection. They simply must have this unconditional love to cope most effectively in today's world. Being close to mother is very reassuring to the baby. In the biological program of mother and baby there are certain built-in guarantees

> for the satisfaction of the baby's needs that ensure the formation of human bonds in the first eighteen months of life. The mother is the primary need satisfier, and that need satisfaction should lead the infant through a series of stages in the first year in which the mother is loved more than any other person in his small world. What your baby needs most of all is his mother. No one else can take her place. Children's natural values are very human and simple. They want to be comfortable. Given a choice between the warmth of human values and material values, babies will almost always choose the human."[4]

Do you see the significance of this? Because of her love, a mother gives of herself to meet her baby's needs. Thus, it is virtually impossible for a nursing mother to ever forget the love and bonding she had with her baby. I had a friend who went back to her hometown and while there, visited a woman whose 46-year-old son had died. As she visited with this mother, do you know what was one of the fond and meaningful remembrances she had of her son that she talked about? It was when he was a nursing baby. Certainly, no true mother could ever forget her child and have no compassion upon him because of her love. But, even if this could occur, our heavenly Father will never forget His children because His love is much greater than that of a mother.

> The great preacher, D. L. Moody, stated, "The closest tie on earth is a mother's love for her child. There are a good many things that will separate a man from his wife, but there isn't a thing in the wide, wide world that will separate a true mother from her own child. I will admit that there are unnatural mothers, that there are mothers who have gone out of their heads, mothers who are steeped in sin and iniquity that they will turn against her own child. I have talked with mothers when my blood boiled with indignation against the sons for their treatment of their mothers, and I have said, 'Why don't you cast him off?' They have said, 'Why, Mr. Moody, I love him still. He is my son.'"[5]

Then Moody shared a story from a fellow pastor whom he had preached for while visiting St. Louis which illustrates this great truth. There was a boy that was very bad and this was a result of his having a bad father who delighted in teaching his son everything that was bad. After the father died, the son's behavior got even worse until he was arrested for murder. During the trial, it was learned that he had murdered five other people. This led to a universal cry from the city against him. The outrage against him was so extreme that during the trial they had to guard the courthouse. As the trial was being conducted, the mother got as close as she could to her son. With every witness testifying against her son, it hurt her more than it did her son. When the jury gave a verdict of guilty, a great shout went out from the people, but the mother nearly fainted. When the judge announced that the guilty defendant would be sentenced to death, the people thought that the mother would faint away.

When the trial was over the mother threw her arms around her son and kissed him. In fact, she held him so tightly that they had to tear him from her embrace. She then went throughout the city trying to get the men to sign a petition for his pardon. Of course, her efforts were futile. When the son was executed by hanging, she begged the governor for his body so that she might bury it. Even though death may tear down everything in the world, it cannot tear down a mother's love. The governor refused, but the mother continued to cherish the memory of her son. A few months later the mother was at the point of death and she made one final request of the governor. She wanted to be buried next to her son. That depicts a mother's love. This mother was not ashamed to have her grave pointed out as the grave of the mother of the most noted criminal ever in the state of Vermont.[6] Here again, let's focus on the words of Isaiah 49:15ab, "Can a woman forget her nursing child, And have no compassion on the son of her womb?" As great as a true mother's love is for her child, it cannot be compared to the heavenly Father's love for His children.

This is further clarified by what is written in Isaiah 49:16a. Using an anthropomorphic figure, God's hands, it is as if God has inscribed His children on the palms of His hands. It was the custom of that day for men to place tattoos on their arms of those things that meant the most to them, whether it was their gods, family members, or some object. The further down the arm, the more important that person or object was to them.[7] Do you see the significance of verse 16a? God's children are the furthermost thing down His arm and thus, the most important to Him. Therefore, whenever our Father does anything with His hands, continuing the anthropomorphic figure, He does it with His children in full view, thinking of them at all times. As Dean Plumtre said, "Our Father cannot act without being reminded of His children."[8] And Gardiner Spring wrote, "Whom He loves, He loves to the end. Heaven and earth shall pass away, but this faithful word of love and mercy shall never pass away."[9]

So, our heavenly Father loves His children unconditionally. Not only does our Father love us unconditionally, He also loves us uniquely. Joanie Yoder wrote a devotional entitled, "God's Favorites." In her devotional, she stated that when her first daughter was born she loved her so much that she was afraid when she had another child she might not love that child as much. When her second daughter was born, however, she realized that she loved her as much as the first daughter, yet uniquely. The spiritual lesson Joanie learned from her experience was that God loves each of His children completely without taking love away from any of His other children. Thus, when we come to Him, as His children, we have His complete attention. Joanie then wrote about those who warn us against acting as if our heavenly Father has favorites. She once heard a preacher state, "Of course God has favorites! We're all His favorites!"[10]

Every principle in this book is important, but I believe that this principle of parents loving their children unconditionally is of extreme importance. Why? I believe all the other principles stem or flow from our unconditional love for our children. This is also true of our heavenly Father. Ephesians 1:4c-5a states, "In love He predestined us to adoption as sons through Jesus Christ to Himself." And why did God send Jesus to earth? John 3:16 says it was because He so loved us and Romans 5:8 states that He did it to demonstrate His love for us even while we were yet sinners. Now, why does our heavenly Father discipline His children? As we saw from Hebrews 12:6a which comes from Proverbs 3:12, "For those whom the LORD loves He disciplines." As Thomas Watson wrote, "If God be a Father, then whatever He does to His children is in love."[11] So, parents' unconditional love for their children is shown as we provide for them, teach them, discipline them, etc. Now, you would think that this principle is one that we would not have to emphasize much, but sadly that is not the case. We are seeing more and more parents that truly don't love their children unconditionally. Of course, that is obvious with the many child abusers in our society and those parents that have even murdered their own children, but it extends even further than those two examples. Many years ago, Ann Landers received the following letter.

Dear Ann Landers:

"A year ago our two-year-old son, Earl, had difficulty breathing so we took him to a doctor. We learned Earl is allergic to cigarette smoke. My husband said we both had to quit smoking right then and there. He hasn't touched a cigarette since. I went back to smoking that same night.

"I don't smoke when little Earl is in the room and it's awfully hard on me. My husband doesn't know I smoke so I make excuses to go to the basement or out in the garage whenever I want a cigarette. Sneaking around is making me nervous.

"Do you think it would be wrong if we let a nice couple adopt little Earl- a nice couple who don't smoke? Then I could smoke in the open and my husband could take it up again, too.

"The only problem is that my husband is crazy about the boy. I love him, too, but I am more the practical type. What do you think Ann? Mrs. E.R.M."

Ann's response was:

Dear Mrs. E.R.M.

"I think a lot of people who read this letter are going to say I made it up. It's utterly fantastic that a mother would put cigarettes ahead of her own child.

"Don't present your wild idea to your husband. I wouldn't blame him if he decided to keep little Earl and unload YOU."[12]

Did you notice that the mother wrote that she loved Earl, but clearly she didn't love him with an unconditional type love. She loved herself and her cigarettes more than she loved her own son. Many parents are depicting the same thing today. They depict a love for themselves more than their children through gambling, drugs or alcohol. Many parents' actions depict they love their jobs more than they love their children. Oh, they may say they are working hard to provide for their children, but the reality is a love for their job and the material things it can provide for the parents also. And parents whose focus is on jobs, money and material possessions are displaying a wrong priority to their children. I know of a lady who was talking with two children in the age range of 8-10. They came from a Christian family, but the family also appeared to be materialistic. This became more evident when the lady asked the children what was the most important thing the parents could give them. She was hoping that the children would say "love", but sadly they said "money". In chapter 4, I used a quote from Mike Singletary of fathers who may need to rethink accepting promotions or job transfers for the sake of their children. He concludes that thought with these words, "More important than providing a life of ease for your kids is making sure they know you love them unconditionally."[13]

Even though we are witnessing more and more parents whose love is growing cold toward their children, still a large percentage of parents, and especially Christian parents, do love their children unconditionally. At the same time, however, parents need to be careful that their actions don't communicate to their children a love that is conditional. As stated in a previous chapter, our words can often depict this, but I want to address two areas that were mentioned in focusing on our heavenly Father's unconditional love for His children.

First, just as our heavenly Father's unconditional love for His children is not based on our performance, parents should seek to make sure that they communicate the same thing to their children. In the previous chapter, I mentioned an example of even grown children having to perform or act in a particular way or the parent gets upset. And I stated that the bottom line is that the relationship is really based on performance rather than unconditional love. I want to expand upon this now. The best way I can illustrate this is by sharing an episode from my favorite all time television show, the black and white version of "The Andy Griffith Show." If you watched that show, you may remember that Andy's son, Opie, was not the best student in school. In one episode, Opie was home with Aunt Bee waiting anxiously for his Paw to come home. When Andy came home he sat down and Opie gave him his report card. Andy opened it with hesitation, obviously fearful of what he would see. As he read the report card, however, he saw that Opie had made straight A's. Andy got so excited and said to Aunt Bee, "What are we going to do to reward a boy like this?" Aunt Bee told Andy that she had already made his favorite pie. So, they were all in quite a celebratory mood because of Opie's performance in school.

The next day at school, Opie's teacher, Miss Crump, asks him to come to her desk. She tells Opie that she had made a mistake when transcribing the grades. He had not made all A's, but in fact had even failed arithmetic. Opie was extremely disappointed and after school, goes home and proceeds straight to his room. When Andy comes home later that afternoon he brings a brand new bike to surprise Opie. He brings it into the house and hides it behind the couch. He then calls for Opie to come downstairs. Andy tells Opie that he had left his slippers behind the couch and wanted Opie to get them for him. When Opie goes behind the couch, he then sees the brand new bike. Andy asks him what he thinks of it and with a big smile on his face, Opie says, "Neat." Then, however, Andy says to Opie, "Did you ever know a father that had more reason to be proud of his son than I do with you getting all A's?" The smile on Opie's face turned to sadness and rather than riding his new bike, he states that he wants to go back to his room and study.

The next day, Opie comes to the Sheriff's office and tells his Paw that he wanted to talk with him about something. Before he gives Opie a chance to say anything, Andy states that he knows what Opie wanted to say. Opie probably wanted an advance on his allowance, which

Andy quickly gave him. He then asks Opie if he had ridden his bike to the Sheriff's office. When Opie says that he hadn't, Andy then says to Opie, "Take it and ride it. After all, you earned it, didn't you? Opie, go ahead and ride the bike. You deserve it, getting all those A's."

After supper that night, Opie again tries to talk to his Paw about his grades, but Andy couldn't listen then because he was going to help Aunt Bee with the dishes. As Andy helps Aunt Bee, with Opie listening in the background, Andy tells Aunt Bee that she should have heard the boys at the barber shop after he had told them about Opie getting all A's. He then states that he was so proud of Opie. In fact, he was considering taking Opie to town and getting a picture of him with his report card and then sending it to another man who always bragged about his children's grades.

The next day, Miss Crump comes by the Sheriff's office to see Andy. Andy told her how surprised and proud he was of Opie for making straight A's. Miss Crump said, "Didn't Opie tell you?" She then explained that Opie had not made straight A's, but had made some low grades and even failed arithmetic. Andy goes home immediately and calls for Opie to come downstairs. There was no response. So, Andy goes to Opie's room and finds a note on his bed that he had run away. Andy goes searching for Opie and finds him walking on a dirt road outside of town. Andy asks Opie where he was going. Opie said, "I'm going away to some place and not come back till I do something to make you proud of me again. I might as well tell you because you will find out. I didn't get all A's. I wanted to tell you, but knew how awful disappointed you would be. So, I thought the best thing to do was run away and come back when you could be proud of me again." Then Andy said to Opie, "Opie, I need to tell you something. When I thought you got all A's, I made it so important that it was impossible for you to live up to it. You're my son and I'm proud of you just for that. You do the best you can and that is fine with me." What was Andy telling Opie? I love you because you're my son and it has nothing to do with your grades (performance in school).

Please understand, I'm not saying that parents shouldn't encourage or challenge their children to be the best they can be in every aspect of life. What I am saying, though, is this. We are to be careful that our words and actions don't depict to our children that we appear to love them differently based on their performance in school, athletics, etc.

Then secondly, as demonstrated perfectly with our heavenly Father, parents should seek to love their children uniquely. I once heard a story about a man who had several children and someone asked him if one of his children was his favorite. He stated, "Yes," and then proceeded to share an experience he had with this particular child and closed by saying, "So, I guess he is my favorite." Then, however, he quickly stated, "But there was that time with my daughter" and related a special experience he had shared with her. Then he said, "So, I guess she is my favorite." Here again though, he states, "But there was that time with my other son," and proceeds to relate an experience with him and then, as before, said, "So, I guess he is my favorite." The father follows this same type of conversation until he has mentioned every one of his children. As was described in the devotional by Joanie Yoder concerning our heavenly Father, all of this father's children were his favorites. He loved them uniquely. He knew their individual struggles and successes and was always there to love them the way they needed to be loved. What some of our children struggle with, our other children may not face those struggles, but have different struggles of their own. We need to treat them all as if each one of them was our favorite. Let's recall what we saw in Chapter 1 reference Jacob and his sons. Genesis 37:3-4 clearly states that Joseph was his favorite son whom he loved more than all of his other sons which resulted in the brothers hating Joseph. How do you think the brothers would have felt about Joseph if they had all been treated as favorites by Jacob? Probably much different than what they did.

An evangelist was once asked, "If your son was a homosexual, would you still love him?" The evangelist's response was, "I'd try to love him even more." No. The evangelist would not condone his son's sinful behavior, but in his concern for the son's spiritual and physical well-being, he would seek to demonstrate love for him uniquely in a way that would not be necessary with his other children.

Another way that we can love our children uniquely is by knowing what they truly enjoy doing, and then participating with them in those areas of interest. A friend of mine with two sons once told me that one son really liked to play golf, while the other son really enjoyed going to different restaurants to eat. Thus, with one son, the dad would play golf and with the other son, they would go out to eat together. What was the father doing? Showing unique love to both sons and treating them both as if they were his favorites.

One of my favorite chapters in the Bible is Romans 8. It speaks of there being no condemnation to those who are in Christ Jesus. As we saw in Chapter 1, Romans 8 speaks of the spirit of adoption that we have received whereby we can cry out, "Abba! Father!" It speaks of the redemption of our bodies. It speaks of the Holy Spirit interceding for us. It speaks of our heavenly Father being for us. So many great promises and blessings for the child of God are mentioned in this chapter. This magnificent chapter closes out with the following words,

> "Who shall separate us from the love of Christ? Shall tribulation, or distress, or persecution, or famine, or nakedness, or peril, or sword? Just as it is written, 'FOR THY SAKE WE ARE BEING PUT TO DEATH ALL DAY LONG; WE WERE CONSIDERED AS SHEEP TO BE SLAUGHTERED.' But in all these things we overwhelmingly conquer through Him who loved us. For I am convinced that neither death, nor life, nor angels, nor principalities, nor things present, nor things to come, nor powers, nor height, nor depth, nor any other created thing, shall be able to separate us from the love of God, which is in Christ Jesus our Lord."
> —v. 35-39

What a blessed truth for a child of God to know that he or she is loved unconditionally and that no circumstances in life can separate us from His love. I mentioned previously Watson's quote, "If God be a Father, then whatever He does to His children is in love." And we saw from Isaiah 49:16a, it is as if God has inscribed His children upon the palms of His hands. Thus, whatever comes from our sovereign Father's hands, in other words, our circumstances, whether it be tribulation, distress, persecution, famine, nakedness, peril, or sword, are filtered through His fingers of unconditional love. And it is His perfect love, which casts out fear (1 John 4:18), that enables us to overwhelmingly conquer in the midst of those difficult circumstances that we experience in life.

David McCasland wrote a devotional for Thanksgiving Day, 2002, entitled, "Unfailing Love." He wrote about a scene that retired pastor Browning Ware, shared with some close friends after visiting his wife in a residence for Alzheimer's patients. Ware stated: "We shared hugs all around and held hands in prayer. So much to be grateful for! I thanked God for family, for friends, and for His radical love that liberates us even when caught within life's clawing circumstances." McCasland then wrote, "As we pause to thank God for every way He has blessed us, it's good to remember that our greatest treasure is His unfailing love. Too often our thankfulness ebbs and flows with our health or financial security. We equate God's blessing with freedom from pain and sorrow. But through faith and experience we learn that God's great love for us expressed in Jesus Christ can calm our hearts and minds even in the most taxing situations...It is not health or wealth, but God's unfailing love that sets us free in every circumstance of life."[14]

Knowing and then living that great truth enables us to face life with confidence and consequently, without fear. Parents, when we love our children unconditionally and unfailingly, it will be easier for them to accept some of the difficult decisions we may have to make for them in their formative years which they may not like initially, but in the long run, they will appreciate and respect us for. In addition to this, they will be better equipped to face life with confidence knowing they are loved unconditionally. This also provides a great deal of security for them as they grow and experience other challenges in life.

Chapter Ten

Praying for Your Children

Hence, also, He is able to save forever those
who draw near to God through Him, since
He always lives to make intercession for them.
—Hebrews 7:25

And in the same way the Spirit also helps our
weakness; for we do not know how to pray as
we should, but the Spirit Himself intercedes for
us with groanings too deep for words; and He
who searches the hearts knows what the mind
of the Spirit is, because He intercedes for the
saints according to the will of God.
—Romans 8:26-27

Pray without ceasing;
—1 Thessalonians 5:17

"and give to my son Solomon a perfect heart
to keep Thy commandments, Thy testimonies,
and Thy statutes, and to do them all,"
—1 Chronicles 29:19a

As we examine this final lesson or principle for parents in raising their children, which is prayer, it may be the most important. Now you may think that I'm contradicting myself with what I stated in the previous chapter for I wrote of the extreme importance of parents loving their children unconditionally. In reality, however, I don't believe you can separate prayer and love because one of my favorite definitions of prayer is "love on its knees." Why then is parents praying for their children the most important lesson or principle? One reason is depicted in a statement by one of the Wesley brothers, either John or Charles, if I remember correctly. One of them stated that "God does nothing but in answer to prayer." Another reason that prayer is so important is that it is the one thing you can do when you can't do the other lessons that have been discussed in this book. Do you remember my friend whom I mentioned as stating there are times "when you must put your children on the altar." In essence, she was saying the only thing she could do for her children at that time was pray for them. They weren't receptive to anything she tried to do for them as it related to the Lord, but she could pray for them, and pray for them she did. Think of the prodigal son when he was in the far country. The father could not provide for him any further or teach him or discipline him, etc. but he could sure pray for him and even though that was not mentioned in the parable, you would surely assume that a loving, compassionate, gracious father did just that. Then there are those numerous times in which children leave home to go off to school, the military, the mission field, or a job in another area. Parents often feel like they can't do much for their children in such instances, but one thing they can do is pray.

In the previous chapters, we have used Scriptures which compare our heavenly Father to earthly fathers or mothers to illustrate some principle of parenting whereby we can seek to imitate Him and thus, be better parents to our children. When we come to this principle of prayer, however, there is no Scripture which speaks of our heavenly Father praying for His children as an earthly parent would. Of course, that makes sense because our heavenly Father is the recipient of prayer and thus, He would not pray to Himself. At the same time, however, we need to realize that we do have God praying for His children. God the Son and God the Holy Spirit pray for us and that is the emphasis of the Hebrews and Romans passages that introduced this chapter. Therefore, we will examine those passages as they relate to the principle of prayer whereby parents can learn how to more effectively pray for their children.

First of all, let's focus on Jesus praying for us as recorded in Hebrews 7:25. One of the most exalted positions within Judaism was that of the High Priest. In fact, that was one of the reasons that many Jews of the first century had a problem with Christianity. Whereas Judaism had a High Priest, they felt that Christianity had no High Priest. Nothing could be further from the truth. When the Jews thought of their High Priest, what did they think of? They thought of a mediator for them who would once a year enter the Holy of Holies with blood to sprinkle in front of and on the mercy seat to make atonement for their sins. In this, however, we see how limited the High Priest was for he could never fully bring a person to God. We know from Scripture that the Holy of Holies pointed to the presence of God. There was a veil which separated the Holy of Holies from the Holy Place. And only the High Priest could enter within the veil and that was only once a year. So, there was always a barrier which prevented the people from entering God's presence. That barrier could not be removed because sin had not truly been taken away for as Hebrews 10:4 states, "for it is impossible for the blood of bulls and goats to take away sins." The author of Hebrews, though, writes that Christians do have a High Priest, Jesus Christ, Who is much superior to any High Priest under Judaism for He did what they could not do. The veil or barrier was removed because He perfectly atoned for sin whereby a child of God can enter the presence of God and draw near to Him as their loving Father.

Another reason that Jesus is a superior High Priest is that He holds His priesthood permanently. Hebrews 7:23 states that the priests under the Levitical priesthood existed in greater numbers. In other words, there were numerous priests under the Old Covenant.

Why? Because they were prevented by death from continuing their priestly functions. Think of the first High Priest, Aaron. In Numbers 20, God tells Moses to take Aaron and his son, Eleazar, up to Mount Hor. Aaron was stripped of his priestly garments and they were put on his son. Then Aaron died (v.26-28). Obviously, Aaron could not continue being the priest and the responsibility was passed on to his son. Thus, priests had to continually be replaced.

What about Jesus? Hebrews 7:24, concerning Jesus' priesthood, is a definite contrast with what was written in verse 23. Because He abides forever, He holds His priesthood permanently. The word "permanently" is a legal word. It means non-transferable. So, it would speak of that which belongs to a person and can never be taken away. As it relates to Jesus then, His priesthood can never be taken from Him and transferred to someone else. He has no successor and thus, He is the last High Priest and there will never be another one needed.

Consequently, Hebrews 7:25 instructs us of the significance of what it means that He holds His priesthood permanently. Due to the emphasis of this chapter on prayer, we primarily want to focus on the last part of the verse. It is important, however, to briefly examine the first part of the verse in order to better understand the last part of the verse. Verse 25a tells us, "He is able to save forever those who draw near to God through Him." The phrase "able to save" means that He has the power to save. And the word "forever" actually means to the uttermost or completely. This Greek word is only used here and in Luke 13:11, where it refers to the woman who could not straighten herself completely. So, Jesus, as a permanent High Priest, is able to save completely which refers to the entire salvation process. He has the power to save from the penalty of sin (justification), from the power and pleasure of sin (sanctification), and from the presence of sin (glorification).

Then we read that He is able to save completely those who draw near to God through Him. This refers to those who truly believe in Him as demonstrated by their repentance from sin and faith in His finished work at Calvary on their behalf. And when a person truly draws near to God through Jesus, his life will reflect that as he seeks to faithfully obey the Scriptures. Ezekiel Hopkins wrote, "God hath instituted the way of salvation to be by the death of Christ, who hath appointed the virtue of His death to be applied to us only by the grace of faith; which faith, without obedience and good works, is in itself dead, and can never justify or save us."[1] If a person then tries to draw near to God through any other person or efforts of their own apart from Jesus, then Jesus is not able to save them completely.

Why is Jesus able to save completely all those who draw near to God through Him? Because He always lives to make intercession for them. The word "intercession" speaks of presenting petitions in behalf of another. In other words, Jesus is praying for God's children. As we think on Jesus praying for us, there are three great truths to consider. The first truth is to realize that Jesus' intercession is to be considered in a two-fold aspect. First, let's focus on His intercession in His state of humiliation. In other words, while He was still on earth prior to His crucifixion. John 17 records Jesus' High Priestly Prayer, which is really the true Lord's Prayer. That prayer can be broken down into three parts. He prayed for Himself, His disciples at that time, and then for all who would ever be believers in Him. John 17:24ab records Jesus praying, "Father, I desire that they also, whom Thou hast given Me, be with Me where I am, in order that they may behold My glory, which Thou hast given Me." What was He praying? That their salvation would be complete in that they would be with Him in glory. Then when He was on the cross, He interceded, "Father, forgive them; for they do not know what they are doing." Never forget, Jesus was despised and rejected of men. He was accursed of God and yet, He still interceded. Hopkins wrote, "when He was under the sharpest agonies; when He was bruised by God and broken by men, suffering the wrath of the one, and the wrongs of the other; when His own pains might have made His prayers selfish, or His enemies' malice might have made Him revengeful: yet, even then, He forgets not to intercede for them."[2] If you are a Christian, it is because the Father answered these prayers of Jesus. There is a song that I often listen to which says, "When He was on the cross, I was on His mind" and I believe that as He interceded for me.

The second aspect of Jesus' intercession deals with the context of verse 25 in that He is interceding on our behalf in His state of exaltation and glory. As Jesus is on the throne at the right hand of the Father, He is there as our Mediator and Advocate. John wrote in 1 John 2:1, "My little children, I am writing these things to you that you may not sin. And if anyone sins, we have an Advocate with the Father, Jesus Christ the righteous." So, when God's children sin, Jesus is at the right hand of the Father to intercede for us. Paul wrote in Romans 8:33-34, "Who will bring a charge against God's elect? God is the one who justifies; who is the one who condemns? Christ Jesus is He who died, yes, rather who was raised, who is at the right hand of God, who also intercedes for us." Something else to realize regarding Jesus in heaven interceding for us. When Israel's High Priest would enter the Holy of Holies, part of the priestly garments that he wore was a breastpiece. This breastpiece had twelve stones on it corresponding to the names of the sons of Israel. And each stone was engraved with the engravings of a signet with the name for the twelve tribes (Exodus 39:14). Jesus, in heaven, now has the names of His own in His heart as He goes to the Father to pray for us. Thomas Goodwin wrote of Christians, "We are God's jewels, precious in His own account and choice. So that God loves us as jewels chosen by Him, but much more when He beholds us set and presented unto Him in the breastplate of Christ's heart and prayer."

The second truth related to Jesus praying for us is to realize that He is not pleading for us in the presence of a reluctant God, but a loving Father. In the previous paragraph, I mentioned Romans 8:33-34, but recall what Romans 8:31-32 says, "What then shall we say to these things? If God is for us, who is against us? He who did not spare His own Son, but delivered Him up for us all, how will He not also with Him freely give us all things?" Did you notice that God is for us and that was shown by His delivering up His

Son for us. Hopefully each chapter of this book has demonstrated, Jesus did not die on the cross to make the Father love those who would be His children, but because He did love them. Jesus does not continually pray for God's children to force the Father to give us what we need, but because He delights to freely give us all things. As H. B. Swete wrote, "Jesus is a throned Priest-king, asking what He will from a Father who always hears and grants His request."[3]

The final truth reference Jesus praying for God's children is the encouragement it is for his children. There are two words of encouragement that are important to understand. In order to understand the first word of encouragement, I need to ask a few questions. Do you ever feel that your faith is weak? Do you ever feel like you are just messing up all the time in your Christian walk? Do you ever feel that you are so bombarded by Satan, the flesh and the world that you'll never be victorious over their temptations and assaults? Do you ever feel like you are such a disappointment to your heavenly Father? Beloved, Jesus always lives to make intercession for you.

We've looked at this passage previously, but a great example of this which ought to encourage believers centers around Peter's great boast that he was ready to go to prison and to death for Christ (Luke 22:33). What was the context of his making such a boast? In Luke 22:31-32, Jesus tells Peter, "Simon, Simon, behold, Satan has demanded permission to sift you like wheat; but I have prayed for you, that your faith may not fail; and you, when once you have turned again, strengthen your brothers." In Peter's boast, it was as if Peter was saying, "Lord, You don't need to pray about my faith failing because I'm ready to die for you." Jesus, however, had prayed for Peter even when Peter didn't know that he needed prayer. And do you realize, that prayer was answered. Peter did turn again and strengthened the brothers. Just think of Pentecost. That great event occurred less than eight weeks after Peter's denials of Christ, even with cursings. As stated in Chapter 7, probably most of us would have never chosen Peter to preach the sermon at Pentecost which resulted in the salvation of three thousand souls. Yet, God chose him and I believe it was in answer to Jesus' prayer for Peter.

The example of Peter illustrates the truth of Hebrews 7:25. We saw that Jesus is able to save forever or completely, referring to the entire salvation process, which concludes in eternal glory. And that process includes many trials, tribulations, sufferings, successes, heartaches, mountains and valleys. Through it all, though, Jesus is continually praying for His own until we reach heaven in His glorious presence. He doesn't get tired of interceding for us. The Scottish minister Robert Murray McCheyne stated, "If I could hear Christ praying for me in the next room, I would not fear a million enemies. Yet distance makes no difference. He is praying for me!"[4] How this ought to encourage believers in Him.

A second word of encouragement deals with our own prayers that we offer to our Father. Have you ever felt that your prayers were so inadequate and feeble? I know I have. Chrysostom, a great fourth century preacher, gives a beautiful analogy as it relates to Jesus as our intercessor. There was a young boy whose father was away on a trip. He wanted to present his father with something upon his return home. His mother told him to go to the garden and gather some flowers. When the boy returned from the garden, there were numerous weeds mixed in with the flowers. When the father returned, however, he was presented only with beautiful flowers. The mother had intervened and removed all the weeds.[5] Child of God, as we pray, our prayers may be like that. Many weeds mixed among a few flowers. When they are taken to the Father as a result of Jesus' intercession, they are beautiful flowers. Jesus, the Christian's Great High Priest, holds His priesthood permanently and always lives to pray for those who draw near to God through Him.

Not only does God the Son pray for God's children, but as Paul wrote in Romans 8:26-27, God the Holy Spirit also prays for them. The context of these verses is the hope Christians have as they wait eagerly for their adoption as sons, the redemption of their bodies. The redemption of the body speaks of the full or complete adoption as sons, at which time our bodies, which are characterized by sin and weakness, will be redeemed and thus, become imperishable and immortal. That is the Christian's hope and this hope does not refer to just a possibility, but a certainty. The reason that hope is mentioned is that the reality of it is still in the future. As Romans 8:24 states, "Hope that is seen is not hope." Until that hope becomes a reality, we are to wait eagerly for it with perseverance. What does perseverance point to? It points to holding on or remaining steadfast or enduring. It speaks of not swerving from the faith even amidst the greatest trials. The Bible teaches that before hope becomes reality, the redemption of our bodies, we will face tremendous trials and sufferings. As we've already seen from Acts 14:22, "Through many tribulations we must enter the kingdom of God." And 2 Timothy 3:12 states, "And indeed, all who desire to live godly in Christ Jesus will be persecuted." Earlier in Romans 8, Paul had written that the sufferings we will experience are nothing compared to the glory that awaits us, but in the midst of tremendous trials, we may begin to doubt if we will persevere until the glory. The truth of the matter is this. A true child of God will persevere. Why? Because he has an Advocate, a Comforter, the Holy Spirit, Who lives within to help him. That is the emphasis of Romans 8:26-27. Yes, Christians are to be active in their perseverance but we must also realize that the Holy Spirit even more so is active in their perseverance as He intercedes for them. Let's examine then what He does for us based on these verses.

The first thing we see is the help the Holy Spirit gives us. Verse 26 starts out, "And in the same way the Spirit also helps our weakness." The words "in the same way" mean "in like manner." They are a link with what was stated in the previous verses. In the midst of trials and sufferings, what sustains us as we seek to persevere? The hope. Consequently, from verse 26, Paul would be making the connection that in the same way that hope sustains the Christian in the midst of sufferings, so does the Spirit. In reality, though, the Spirit sustains us more than our hope, for our hope may waver, but the Spirit never will. Then we notice what He does. He helps our weakness. The word "help" is made up of three Greek words, "sun," "anti," and "lumbano." The word "sun" means along with or together with. The word "anti" means for or in the place of. The word "lumbano" means to take, to take hold of or to bear. Putting all three of these words together, help then means a coming alongside to take part of the heavy load and help bear it. The word is used in Luke 10 when Jesus was with Martha and Mary. The passage states that Mary was listening to the Lord's words, seated at His feet. Martha, though, was distracted with all her preparations. So, Martha said to Jesus in Luke 10:40b, "Lord, do You not care that my sister has left me to do all the serving alone? Then tell her to help me." What was Martha really saying? "Lord, all these preparations are a heavy load, too much for me to bear alone. Tell Mary to come alongside me to help bear it." When we think of this, our hearts may recall the great invitation of our Lord in Matthew 11. Jesus stated in Matthew 11:28-30, "Come to Me, all who are weary and heavy-laden, and I will give you rest. Take My yoke upon you, and learn from Me, for I am gentle and humble in heart; and YOU SHALL FIND REST FOR YOUR SOULS. For My yoke is easy, and My load is light." What is Jesus saying in that invitation? You are weary and heavy-laden because the load you are trying to carry is too heavy for you. Be yoked to Me and we will walk and perform the labor together. Then you will see that the yoke is easy and the load is light. That is what we are talking about in Romans 8:26 with the Holy Spirit. As we seek to persevere through the trials and sufferings of this present life, the Holy Spirit comes to bear our burdens. And the word "helps" is in the present tense which speaks of a continuous action. Thus, the Holy Spirit comes along to continuously help God's children.

Well, how does He help us? In our weakness. The word "weakness" does not refer to sin but in the context of the Scripture it refers to a lack of knowledge. What is the lack of knowledge that we have? In how to pray, for Paul writes that we don't know how to pray as we should. In order to understand what Paul is saying, there are three important observations that need to be made. First, this does not teach that the child of God has no responsibility whatsoever. This is not a "Let go and let the Spirit" type thing. What did we learn that the Spirit does? He comes alongside to help. He gives us a helping hand, you may say. Remember the context. We are talking about persevering until the redemption of the body. So then, what can we do? James 5:13a states, "Is anyone among you suffering? Let him pray." Therefore, in the midst of our suffering, we are to pray, but what is the reality as we pray? We don't really know how to pray as we should. A man by the name of Gifford wrote, "The Greek adverb does not refer to the manner of praying, but to the correspondence between the prayer and that which is really needed." And John MacArthur wrote, "Because of our imperfect perspectives, finite minds, human frailties and spiritual limitations, we are not able to pray in absolute consistency with God's will. Many times we are not even aware that spiritual needs exist, much less know how best they should be met."[6] Yes, our main responsibility as we seek to persevere, especially in the midst of suffering, is to pray but we are limited and weak as we do so.

The second observation is to focus on how the Holy Spirit comes in to help. Paul writes that He intercedes for us with groanings too deep for words. The word "intercedes" means to plead for someone. The word "groaning" means sighings. And the phrase "too deep for words" means not expressed in words. A. T. Robertson says this speaks of a rescue by one who "happens on" another who is in trouble and "in behalf" pleads with "unuttered groanings" or with "sighs that baffle words."[7] When Paul mentions too deep for words, he is not referring to unspoken or unintelligible words, but words which cannot be grasped in human words but are clearly understood by the Father. In 2 Corinthians 12:4, Paul writes that he was caught up into Paradise. And what did he experience? He heard inexpressible words which a man is not permitted to speak. That could very well be what this refers to. Now, there is a question as to who does the groaning? Is it the Christian or the Spirit? Some commentators state that it is inconceivable for the Godhead to groan. There are two main reasons, however, as to why I believe the Spirit is the one who groans. First, the context of the Scripture. In verse 22 Paul had written of creation groaning and in verse 23 he had written of Christians also groaning. So, in verse 26 it would appear that this is the conclusion concerning the groaning, from creation to the Christian to the Spirit of God. A second reason this refers to the Spirit deals with the Spirit helping the child of God. As mentioned previously, the word "help" refers to coming alongside to bear a heavy load. Let's put this on the practical level. Have you ever helped someone carry a real heavy load? If so, was your conversation formal in that you said something like, "My, what a heavy load that we are burdened with." Probably not. Rather, you probably groaned and staggered until you put the load in its place. Please understand. I'm not saying that any burden is too heavy for the Spirit of God. The point is this. He comes alongside to help.[8] Just as Jesus is described in Hebrews 4:15 as our High Priest who can sympathize with our weakness, we have here the Holy Spirit groaning with us as He intercedes for us.

The third observation is to look at an example from Scripture which hopefully will encourage us. We saw from 2 Corinthians 12 that Paul had been caught up into Paradise. Well, to keep Paul from exalting himself, there was given him a messenger of Satan to buffet him. What did this cause Paul to do? As stated in James 5, he was suffering and thus, went to prayer. He prayed three times that it might depart from him. Did that happen? No. Paul then, as he was seeking to persevere, did not know how to pray as he should. Consequently, the Holy Spirit helped Paul by interceding for him and Paul got the answer that God's grace was sufficient.

Well, what is the result of the Holy Spirit interceding for us? Verse 27 gives the answer. The phrase "He who searches our hearts" refers to our Father. And truly, there are many Scriptures which point to our Father knowing our hearts. Scripture says He alone knows the hearts of men. He searches the hearts and understands every intent of our hearts. He tries the heart and knows the secrets of the heart. What is Paul wanting us to see? Yes, God our Father knows and searches the hearts of men, but even more so He knows the mind of the Spirit. Why? Because the will and mind of the Spirit are the same as the will and mind of the Father. This may seem unnecessary to write such words, but Paul wrote them to encourage believers that the entire Godhead is involved in God's children persevering to glory.

Since the Spirit and the Father are one, what does this mean then as the Spirit intercedes for Christians? Paul writes that He intercedes for Christians according to the will of God. The words "the will of" are in italics which means they are added for clarification. This phrase really says then that the Spirit intercedes for the saints according to God. What is important to realize is that the Spirit always intercedes according to God's will for our lives. When verse 27 speaks of the Spirit interceding for saints according to God's will, this refers to God's sovereign will that involves all aspects of life as He guides us to eternal glory. Yes, the Bible records God's revealed will, which is a part of His sovereign will for our lives, but so much of His sovereign will is hidden from us and thus, not available to be discovered until it has already occurred. That may sound discouraging, but it is not. As James Montgomery Boice wrote, "it is of the greatest importance for us to know that God has a plan for our lives and is directing us in it, particularly when we do not know what it is. It means that we can trust Him and go forward confidently, even when we seem to be walking in the dark, as we so often are."[9]

Consequently, since God's sovereign will for us is hidden in so many areas, we do not need to know it because the Holy Spirit knows it and is praying that for us. That is the emphasis of Romans 8:27 and this ought to be a source of great comfort. The truth is this. Our Father is completely sovereign and His ultimate plan for His children is to bring us to eternal glory. That is what the Holy Spirit is praying for us and since it is God's will, our Father will answer it as 1 John 5:14-15 says. Remember David's words from Psalm 37:23-24, "The steps of a man are established by the LORD; And He delights in his way. When he falls, he shall not be hurled headlong; Because the LORD is the One who holds his hand." Did you notice the phrase "when he falls?" Do you realize that our loving Father has sovereignly ordained our falls? And so many of these falls are extremely painful. The Puritans referred to such as "hard providences." In order to understand this, we must realize that there are two aspects to God's will. There is His revealed will and His sovereign or decreed will. Of course, His revealed will is His word. His decreed or sovereign will is what He has ordained will happen which includes the hidden plans that were mentioned previously. Deuteronomy 29:29 depicts both of these aspects of God's will. "The secret things belong to the LORD our God, but the things revealed belong to us and to our sons forever, that we may observe all the words of this law." As followers of Christ, we are to seek to obey His revealed will. Many times, however, God will allow His revealed will to be broken, but His decreed will will never be broken. Earlier in this chapter we focused on Peter's denials of Christ. Peter's actions violated God's revealed will, but it was a part of His decreed will whereby Peter would eventually strengthen the brethren as Jesus had prayed for him. Let's look at some practical examples of this for the day in which we live.

Suppose you are a faithful, submissive employee as Ephesians, Colossians and 1 Peter instruct us. You are a hard worker and thus, a real witness for Christ through your work ethic. Let's assume your boss decides to fire you or give you a pay cut for no apparent reason or maybe because of your Christian walk. Of course, the boss would be violating God's revealed will of how an employer is to treat his employees, but you need to realize that God had sovereignly decreed you to get fired or take a pay cut. That is part of His plan, your steps that He has established, as He is guiding you to glory. And as Romans 8:28 tells us, God will cause all things to work together for good to those who love Him and are called according to His purpose. A prime example of this in Scripture is Joseph, whom I mentioned earlier. He was falsely accused by Potiphar's wife of sexually attacking her, when in reality, he had obeyed God's word by fleeing when she had made the sexual advance. The false accusation led to Joseph's imprisonment. Joseph's steps were obviously very painful, but they had been decreed by God to eventually preserve the nation of Israel.

A second example is to assume that you begin to feel sick, but you don't feel it is so bad that you need to go the doctor. A month later, though, you still aren't feeling good and when you finally go to the doctor, he tells you that you have a terminal disease and if you had come a month earlier he could have done something, but now it is too late. Do you realize that God has sovereignly ordained the timing of your doctor visit?

Let's consider one final example. Suppose you are faced with a decision and in the process you violate some principles of God's word. Then you suffer or face some hard times as a result of it. Yes, you violated God's word, but all this was a part of our Father's sovereign will and plan for your life. Think of Samson. Judges 14 states that Samson had seen a daughter of the Philistines and told his parents that he wanted them to get her for his wife (v.2). His father and mother said to him, "Is there no woman among the daughters of your relatives, or among all our people, that you go to take a wife from the uncircumcised Philistines?" (v.3a). Samson, however, said to his father, "Get her for me, for she looks good to me" (v.3b). So, Samson's parents knew that his marrying this Philistine woman would violate God's revealed will. Yet, this was according to God's decreed will for verse 4ab states, "However, his father and mother did not know that it was of the LORD, for He was seeking an occasion against the Philistines." Please understand, this is not a license to sin and then just say that was part of God's sovereign will. As Dr. Waltke wrote, "God's providence (decreed will) includes evil and moral ambiguities. It cannot be used to justify wrongdoing."[10] Therefore, we are to always seek to obey His word because we love Him and then trust Him with whatever happens. As I've heard it described before, God's revealed will, His word, is the guide for our lives and His sovereign will is then the diary that we look back at to see how He has directed our steps. That is the point of the Holy Spirit praying for us. He intercedes according to our Father's sovereign will for our lives which is hidden from us. Do you see why our Father hides His sovereign will from us? If we knew what His sovereign will was for us ahead of time, more than likely we would never pray such for ourselves. As Boice wrote, " if the Holy Spirit is praying for us in these areas according to the sovereign and efficacious will of God, we can be confident and quite bold, knowing that this sovereign and efficacious will of God will be done."[11] This ought to comfort us for nothing happens to us in which our Father is taken by surprise.

We've looked at Psalm 73 previously in this book, but I want to reflect on it again because it illustrates this great truth. It is a Psalm of Asaph, which depicts a real struggle that he had, and if most Christians were honest with themselves, it is a struggle that we may have also. Asaph came close to stumbling because he was envious of the arrogant as he saw the prosperity of the wicked (v.2-3). He then reflected on how the wicked seemed to have a life of ease while he, who sought to live righteously, was stricken all day long and chastened every morning (v.14). This was really troublesome to him until he came to the sanctuary of God and perceived their end (v.17). More importantly, however, he realized how blessed he was. He was continually with God because God had taken hold of his right hand (v.23). He also realized that God's counsel would guide him and afterward receive him to glory (v.24). No. Asaph's circumstances may not have changed. His pilgrimage, those steps ordered by God, would include many "hard providences," but afterward, he would go to glory. Our lives will also include many "hard providences" from our loving, sovereign Father and we could not make it through life and thus, to eternal glory if God the Son and God the Holy Spirit were not praying to God the Father on our behalf.

As we have studied about Jesus and the Holy Spirit praying for God's children, this has hopefully been an encouragement and an exhortation to us parents to do the same for our children. I want to emphasize two truths related to our praying for our children as we would seek to imitate Jesus and the Holy Spirit praying for God's children. The first truth is that we should be constantly praying for our children. Paul wrote in 1 Thessalonians 5:17, "pray without ceasing." This verse is sandwiched by two other short but important verses. Paul wrote in 1 Thessalonians 5:16,18, "Rejoice always...in everything give thanks; for this is God's will for you in Christ Jesus." We may often hear that giving thanks in everything is God's will for His children because that is clearly stated. In the context, however, rejoicing always and praying without ceasing are also God's will for His children. The phrase "without ceasing" means without intercession or without interruption. It is a word that was used of that which was continually and repeatedly done. For example, the writings of Josephus state that it was used of repeated military attacks or a regular and consistent production of fruit.

This principle is taught throughout Scripture. Luke 18:1 states of Jesus, "Now He was telling them a parable to show that all times they ought to pray and not to lose heart." And Paul wrote in Ephesians 6:18, "With all prayer and petition pray at all times in the Spirit, and with this in view, be on the alert with all perseverance and petition for all the saints."

Most people don't enjoy going to the dentist, but I do because my dentist, Dr. Glenn DiBartolomeo, is a close friend and dear brother in Christ. We participated in a Crown Ministries Bible Study years ago and whenever I go for my appointment, we always talk about the Lord or His word in some way. During one of my appointments, Glenn shared with me that his daughter was going to Japan on a mission trip for an extended period of time. I told him that I would pray for her. Six months later, when I was back for my next appointment, I asked Glenn how it had gone for his daughter. He stated that it had been great and that God had truly blessed. I then made a statement like, "When our children go off like that, it sure increases our prayer life, doesn't it?" I will never forget Glenn's response. He stated, "Yes, but it shouldn't." And he was exactly right. Our prayers for our children should not depend upon their distance from home or the trials or dangers they may face. Rather, our children need parents who are continually praying for them, regardless of the circumstances.

What does this mean practically? After all, we can't go around moment by moment with our heads bowed and our eyes closed.

So, what does it mean? Let's consider the following question. What does prayer demonstrate or point to? It demonstrates dependence upon God and fellowship with Him or being in His presence. For me, Psalm 16:8a really speaks of the attitude which clarifies this. "I have set the LORD continually before me." So, to pray without ceasing is to be living in the presence of our Father and then, constantly bringing our children's names and needs to our Father. As important as it is to communicate with our children, it is even more important for us to communicate with our Father about our children. And we need to maintain that close fellowship with our Father whereby we can pray without ceasing for our children.

This relates directly then to the next truth regarding praying for our children and that is, what or how are we to pray for them? What did we learn previously about Jesus and the Holy Spirit praying for us? They prayed God's will for our lives. We are to do the same for our children. No. We don't know God's sovereign will to pray for them like Jesus and the Holy Spirit do, but we have plenty to pray for them from God's revealed will, His word. As I have studied Scripture, I have found only one recorded prayer of a parent for his child. It was David's prayer for his son, Solomon, as recorded in 1 Chronicles 29:19. David's prayer for Solomon is in the context of Solomon building the temple for which David had made all the provisions. But what was truly necessary in order for Solomon to complete this great task? David prayed that God would give Solomon "a perfect heart to keep Thy commandments, Thy testimonies, and Thy statutes, and to do them all."

With David's prayer implanted in our thoughts, I want to discuss several prayer requests from God's word that parents should pray for their children. In most cases, I will not mention specifics such as a particular mate, occupation, school, etc. because what we pray for our children in those areas may not be according to His sovereign will as we've previously seen. Please understand though, I am not saying that we should not make specific requests in prayer for our children because we should. Many people keep a journal of specific prayer requests and how God has answered them as an encouragement of His faithfulness in answering prayer. In fact, many of the prayer requests from God's word are specific, as we'll see, and thus, will help us to better know how to pray more specifically for our children concerning particular prayer requests such as a mate, occupation, school, etc. I want to focus on seven prayer requests for our children based upon our Father's revealed will as found in His word.

The first prayer request parents should pray for their children is their salvation. In order for Solomon to keep God's commandments and do them, David first prayed for Solomon a perfect heart. That is the basis for obeying God. Having a new heart, which results in a personal relationship with Jesus Christ as Lord and Savior through repentance of sin and faith in His finished work at Calvary as He experienced God's wrath to pay the penalty for our sin. Ezekiel 36:25-27 describes what God does when He, by His grace, saves a person whereby they are adopted into His family. One of the things He mentions is that He will give a new heart, a heart of flesh, and replace the heart of stone. Therefore, parents should begin praying for the salvation of their children even before pregnancy occurs, but as soon as they are informed of pregnancy, begin praying specifically for that child's salvation. And as we pray for our children's salvation, we should pray that God would save them at an early age. We've already seen from 2 Timothy 3:15 that Timothy knew from childhood the sacred writings which are able to give the wisdom that leads to salvation through faith in Jesus. We should pray that for our children. If parents, however, have become Christians as adults and their children are older, then they should begin praying for their children's salvation immediately after their own salvation.

A second request parents should pray for their children involves their children's friends. Often, when a young person gets in trouble, one of the phrases we may hear is, "He was involved with the wrong crowd." In Proverbs 1:10, Solomon wrote, "My son, if sinners entice you, Do not consent." In the verses that follow he writes of some of those enticements to sin. He then draws a conclusion in Proverbs 1:15 with these instructions, "My son, do not walk in the way with them. Keep your feet from their path." And Paul wrote in 1 Corinthians 15:33, "Do not be deceived: 'Bad company corrupts good morals.'" Therefore, parents should pray that their children will desire the right kind of friends and be protected from the wrong kind of friends. Of course, this does not mean they should have no non-Christian friends for otherwise they could not be a witness to them. Their intimate and close friends, though, the right kind of friends, are those who will encourage and challenge them in their walk with the Lord. Thus, parents should constantly pray for these types of friends for their children.

A third prayer request is that our children will love God and submit to Him rather than submitting to the temptations of their three main enemies, Satan, the world, and their flesh. We know from James 4:7 that as we submit to God and resist the devil, he will flee from us. And Peter describes Satan in 1 Peter 5:8 as a roaring lion, prowling about, seeking someone to devour. Our responsibility then is to resist him, by being firm in our faith. Then we know from Romans 12:2 that the world will seek to conform us to its image which is described in 1 John as the lust of the flesh, the lust of the eyes and the boastful pride of life. Thus, we should pray for our children that they be transformed by the renewing of their mind with God's word as Romans 12:2 also states which will demonstrate that God's will is good, acceptable and perfect. Finally, James 1:14 tells us that we are tempted when we are carried away and enticed by our own lust. Consequently, as we pray this request, we are really praying that our children will love God and hate sin. In that light, we should also pray that our children will hate every false way (Psalm119:104b). Christians are known for hating sins such as abortion, homosexuality and adultery, but are we known for hating such things as gluttony, cheating on our income taxes, gambling or speeding? Please understand, I'm not saying that abortion is the same degree of sin as gluttony, but it should be our desire that our children will hate every false way. And how do they know what the false ways are? Psalm 119:104a says, "From Thy precepts

I get understanding." So, as we pray for our children that they will love God and submit to Him, at the same time we are praying that our children will be students of God's word.

A fourth prayer request is that as our children grow, they will be people of godly character. This is closely related to the previous request but I want to add to it with this request. When I think of this request, I'm reminded of Daniel as recorded in Daniel 6. Daniel was placed in a high government position by pagan king Darius as only one of three commissioners. This upset the other two commissioners and 120 satraps that a Jewish exile held such a high position. So, they sought to find a ground of accusation against Daniel. They could not find any ground of accusation against him except as it related to his obedience to God's law. Therefore, they devised a plan of false loyalty to deceive Darius by having him sign a statute that anyone who made a petition to any god or man besides Darius for thirty days would be thrown into the lion's den. They did this knowing full well that Daniel would continue to pray to his God, the true God, and Daniel didn't disappoint them. When he knew that the document had been signed, he went to his house with the windows open toward Jerusalem and continued kneeling and praying three times a day to his God. Daniel didn't try to hide what he was doing in order to protect himself. We often hear character defined as "doing the right thing when no one else is looking" and that is true. We must realize also that character is "doing the right thing when everyone is looking" even if it means persecution, ridicule or making ourselves look bad in the sight of others. Shadrach, Meshach and Abed-nego displayed the same type character when they refused to bow before Nebuchadnezzar's image and everyone was a witness to it as recorded in Daniel 3. Parents, we need to pray that our children will display that kind of godly character throughout their entire lives.

A fifth prayer request is that our children will marry the right mate. Paul wrote in 2 Corinthians 6:14-15, "Do not be bound together with unbelievers; for what partnership have righteousness and lawlessness, or what fellowship has light with darkness? Or what harmony has Christ with Belial, or what has a believer in common with an unbeliever?" When a marriage consists of a Christian and a non-Christian, it is often called being "unequally yoked." Parents then should pray that their children would be "equally yoked" with another believer. We need to carry this request further, though, for it is possible for two Christians who are married to be "unequally yoked." I read that a young man asked Jonathan Edwards for Edwards' daughter's hand in marriage. Edwards refused, however. The young man pleaded with Edwards because of his love for Edwards' daughter, but Edwards refused. Finally, the young man said, "She is a Christian, isn't she?" Edwards responded that she was a Christian, but she also had a terrible temper. He then stated that the grace of God can live with a person when it would not be wise for that person to live with another person. What did Edwards recognize? Even though the young man and his daughter were both Christians, they would be unequally yoked. When I think of this I'm reminded of David and Jonathan's friendship. First Samuel 18:1 says that their souls were knit together. Thus, parents should pray that their children marry a true soul mate with the same heart's desire to serve their Lord. As parents pray for the right mate for their children, at the same time they should also pray that they remain sexually pure until the marriage bed (1 Corinthians 6:18).

A sixth prayer request is that our children be humble. There are two main reasons for this particular request. First, "GOD IS OPPOSED TO THE PROUD, BUT GIVES GRACE TO THE HUMBLE" (James 4:6). An attitude of pride says that I don't need God while true humility displays sorrow over sin and dependence and trust upon God. One of the most amazing examples of this principle is depicted in the life of Ahab, the most wicked of Israel's kings. First Kings 21 records Ahab coveting Naboth's vineyard. Naboth would not trade or sell his field to Ahab and this really upset him. When Jezebel, Ahab's wicked wife, saw how this upset him, she devised an evil plot that ended in Naboth's death whereby Ahab could have the field. While Ahab was in Naboth's vineyard, the

LORD sent Elijah to him with a message. The LORD's message was one of severe judgment which included: the dogs would lick up his blood where they had licked up Naboth's blood; evil would be brought upon him and he would be utterly swept away; every male from Ahab would be cut off; his house would be made like the house of Jeroboam and Baasha because he had provoked the LORD to anger and caused Israel to sin; the dogs would eat Jezebel in the district of Jezreel; and, the one who belonged to Ahab and died in the city would be eaten by the dogs and the one who died in the field would be eaten by the birds (v. 19-24). So, the LORD's words of judgment to Ahab were severe because there was no one like Ahab who sold himself to do evil (v.25). But when Ahab heard these words from the LORD, verse 27b states, "that he tore his clothes and put on sackcloth and fasted, and he lay in sackcloth and went about despondently." What did Ahab's actions cause the LORD to do? Verse 29 gives the answer in His words to Elijah. "Do you see how Ahab has humbled himself before Me? Because he has humbled himself before Me, I will not bring the evil in his days, but I will bring the evil upon his house in his son's days." Now, if God would show such grace to a wicked, pagan king, won't He, as a loving Father, even more so show it to His children when they humble themselves before Him? A second reason for this prayer request is that humility best characterizes the life of Jesus that Christians are to imitate (Philippians 2:5). And when our children display humility, they will regard others as more important than themselves and will be concerned for the interests of others rather than just their own personal interests (Philippians 2:3-4). This request then is really a prayer that our children will live a life of self-denial. Such a lifestyle is a contrast with the world which focuses on taking care of myself first and foremost. For our children to live humble lives then is a real testimony of God's grace in their lives and should be a request we pray for them.

The final prayer request that I want to mention is that our children, as parents themselves, will faithfully teach their children (our grandchildren) what they have been taught about a relationship with their heavenly Father through Jesus Christ. I mentioned Psalm 78 previously, but I want to reemphasize verses 5-7. "For He established a testimony in Jacob, And appointed a law in Israel, which He commanded our fathers, That they should teach them to their children, That the generation to come might know, even the children yet to be born, That they may arise and tell them to their children, That they should put their confidence in God, And not forget the works of God, But keep His commandments." What was one of the problems that so often occurred in Israel's history? I mentioned this before, but one generation did not faithfully teach the next generation. In the book of Acts we read about the spread of Christianity and churches being established. Yet, as stated previously, there is very little, if any, Christian witness in those areas now. Why? One generation did not faithfully teach the next generation. What have we seen in America's brief history? There was a strong Christian heritage, but today, America is surely not a Christian nation. Why? Children have not been faithfully taught by the previous generation the truths about God from His word. Thus, parents need to continually pray that their children will be faithful in teaching the next generation.

We've examined seven different prayer requests that we, as parents, should pray for our children, but please don't think that I've exhausted the requests. Hebrews 4:12 states that God's word is living and active. Thus, it is always current and has answers to any challenge or opportunity that we may face today or in the future. Did you notice an area of common ground with the seven prayer requests that were mentioned? They were all based upon at least one Scripture and oftentimes, many more. Therefore, parents should search for Scriptures to pray for their children concerning every facet of life for I believe there is a Scripture that applies to whatever our children may be facing. In fact, there are many prayers in Scripture that it would be good for us to pray for our children. Examples of such prayers are: Ephesians 1:16-19a; Ephesians 3:14-19; Philippians 1:9-11; Colossians 1:9b-12; and 2 Thessalonians 1:11-12.

Praying for Your Children

Parents, never forget. "God does nothing but in answer to prayer." As someone stated, "Prayer does not need proof; it needs practice."[12] So, even if you can't do anything for your children, always remember that you can pray. Please don't look at prayer for your children as a last resort when all else fails or when you are powerless to do anything, but as the first resource to call upon your loving, caring, gracious, omnipotent Father to intervene for His glory.

I would like to close this chapter with a poem entitled, "When Father Prays."

> When father prays he doesn't use
> The words the preacher does;
> There's different things for different days,
> But mostly it's for us.
> When father prays the house is still,
> His voice is slow and deep.
> We shut our eyes, the clock ticks loud,
> So quiet we must keep.
> He prays that we may be good boys,
> And later on good men;
> And then we squirm, and think we won't
> Have any quarrels again.
> You'd never think, to look at Dad,
> He once had tempers, too.
> I guess if father needs to pray,
> We youngsters surely do.
> Sometimes the prayer gets very long
> And hard to understand,
> And then I wiggle up quite close,
> And let him hold my hand.
> I can't remember all of it,
> I'm little yet, you see;
> But one thing I cannot forget,
> My father prays for me![13]

Parents, whether your children are little or grown up, do they know you are praying for them?

Epilogue

We hear a lot this day and time about a person's legacy. So often the question is asked, "What will this person's legacy be?" in reference to an athlete, entertainer, explorer, scientist or politician, just to mention a few. I think this is a very important question for parents to consider. Erma Bombeck, a great writer, wrote a column concerning the arguments that occur many times when siblings divide the family inheritance after the parents have died. Too often the children are convinced that they should have a certain item. Bombeck stated that she never wanted any item to remember her parents for she saw their true legacy was the way they lived and not the possessions they left behind.[1]

Parents, what is the legacy you are leaving your children? Dr. Jack McEwen is a friend of mine from years past. He preached the Baccalaureate service when I graduated from high school. He served as a pastor and a dean at a Theological Seminary. He left the Seminary to go to a secular college setting whereby he could be a witness for Christ. His ministry and life have touched numerous lives for Christ and the Kingdom of God. When I served as a Minister of Single Adults in the mid 1980's, I invited him to speak at a Christmas Banquet. He arrived a day early and one of the men in the Single's ministry escorted him to some of the attractions in the Orlando area. This young man had a great time with Dr. McEwen, but the one thing that stood out to him was something Dr. McEwen stated. They were talking about all the ministry opportunities that the Lord had allowed Dr. McEwen to be involved in, but Dr. McEwen stated that the most significant ministry accomplishment for him was that his children would be with him in heaven.

When I think of Dr. McEwen's words, I'm reminded of an e-mail I received entitled "The Starfish" which is paraphrased from "The Star Thrower" by Loren Eiseley. There was a wise man who often went to the ocean to do his writing. One day, as he was walking along the shore, he saw in the distance a human figure moving like a dancer. This intrigued him so he walked faster to catch up. When he got close enough to really see what was happening, he saw that it was a young man. He wasn't dancing, but he was reaching down on the shore, picking up something and gently throwing it back into the ocean. When the man got close enough to speak, he said, "Good morning! What are you doing?" The young man looked up and replied, "Throwing starfish in the ocean." The man then said, "I guess I should have asked, why are you throwing starfish in the ocean?" to which the young man responded, "The sun is up and the tide is going out. And if I don't throw them in they'll die." Realizing how great the task, the man concluded, "But, young man, don't you realize that there are miles and miles of beach and starfish all along it. You can't possibly make a difference!" The young man politely listened and then continued by picking up another starfish and throwing it in the ocean and finally saying, "It made a difference for that one."

When we consider the task of carrying out the Great Commission and getting the gospel to every tribe, language, people and nation, many of us may feel that we could never make a difference. We may feel that we are too insignificant for such a great task. I personally don't believe that is true because God saved each of His children to make a difference and be a witness for Him in various ways. But, even if that were true, parents, the most important difference we can make is in the lives of our children. As someone said, "Our children are the only possessions we can take with us to glory."[2] And Samuel Worcester, in a sermon preached in October 1811 said, "Our children, as well as ourselves, are born for eternity. This world shall pass away, the heavens shall be rolled together like a scroll, the fabric of the universe shall be dissolved; but our children will exist in happiness or in misery, in the realms of light or in the regions of darkness, when the earth and the heavens that now are shall be no more. They are committed to our care to be trained up with reference to their eternal state. As we are faithful or unfaithful, we may be instrumental to their eternal bliss or to their eternal woe!"[3]

I want to address the last sentence of Worcester's words because there may be some Christian parents who have faithfully sought to live out the principles stated in this book and yet, feel like a failure because their children do not love the Lord and aren't interested in spiritual matters. Worcester's words were "we may be instrumental" rather than "we will be successful in bringing them to salvation in the Lord." Please never forget. Regardless of what we do as Christians, God is responsible for the results while we are responsible for faithfulness. What did Paul say in 1 Corinthians 3:5-6 concerning him and Apollos? "What then is Apollos? And what is Paul? Servants through whom you believed, even as the Lord gave opportunity to each one. I planted, Apollos watered, but God was causing the growth." Thus, success in our Father's eyes is not results, but our faithfulness in seeking to be obedient to His revealed will, His word. I think the words of Charles Spurgeon's mother to Charles are very appropriate here. She said, "Charles, your father and I have trained you in righteousness. We have taught you the word of God. We have lived a godly life before you. If you do not live a godly life, we will stand before God in the day of judgment, and bear witness against you!"[4] What was Mrs. Spurgeon saying? She and her husband had been faithful in seeking to be godly parents and that was all God required of them. If Charles rejected the Lord it wouldn't be because they hadn't sought to direct their son to Jesus as his personal Lord and Savior.

Mrs. Spurgeon's words emphasize another important aspect of parenting. A topic that we hear a lot about today is role models for our children. So many children look to athletes or entertainers as their role models. That is OK, to a degree, if that person is a positive influence, but parents are to be the most important role models in their children's lives. Mike Singletary, whom I quoted previously, stated, "I don't mind being a role model. I'm flattered when people say they'd like their kids to be like me. To me, being a role model is a heavy responsibility and a gift from God. I accept it open-heartedly. But at the same time, I don't feel I should become more important in a kid's life than his father and mother. Very few kids ever actually emulate their heroes. They do what their parents did. Parents are the most important role models in their children's lives, for good or bad."[5] Steve Farrar's words further emphasize the truth of what Mike Singletary stated. Farrar said concerning his responsibility as a father, "It is my God-appointed task to ensure that my sons will be ready to lead a family. I must equip them to that end. Little boys are the hope of the next generation. They are the fathers of tomorrow. They must know who they are and what they are to do. They must see their role model in action. That's how they will know what it means to be a male. That puts the ball in my court...and in yours."[6] Farrar's words could also apply to mothers and daughters.

Parents, the key to our fulfilling this great and blessed responsibility is to imitate our heavenly Father and the best way we can do that is by growing in our own relationship with Him. Let me illustrate. There was a great orator who was being honored at a banquet for his great skills. As a part of the evening, this orator recited several of the orations he had done over his career and the result was thunderous applause. Near the end of the banquet, someone requested he recite the 23rd Psalm. He agreed on one condition. That an old pastor friend who was at the banquet would also recite this beloved Psalm. The old pastor reluctantly agreed. The great orator recited the 23rd Psalm and as before, there was thunderous applause. Then the old pastor came to the microphone and in his scratchy voice he recited the Psalm. When he finished, there was no applause, but only tears on the faces of the audience. After the banquet, someone came to the orator to ask him a question. "Why, when you recited the Psalm did everyone applaud and when the old pastor recited it, everyone had tears in their eyes?" The orator stated, "I know the Psalm. He knows the Shepherd." Parents, do you just know about the Father or do you really know the Father? It is my prayer that this book has caused you to reflect on what an awesome Father you have whereby you will long to know Him more intimately and thus, seek to imitate Him in being a parent to your children.

As stated in the Prologue, I am praying that some non-Christians have read this book and as a result, have a longing to be in relationship with God as a loving, gracious Father. If that describes you, won't you call out to Jesus to be merciful to you, the sinner by repenting (turning from) of your sin and by faith trusting in Jesus alone for your salvation through His death at Calvary? Please recall Jesus' great invitation to sinners like you and me as recorded in Matthew 11:28-30. "Come to Me, all who are weary and heavy-laden, and I will give you rest. Take My yoke upon you, and learn from Me, for I am gentle and humble in heart; and YOU SHALL FIND REST FOR YOUR SOULS. For My yoke is easy, and My load is light." Regardless of how great your sin is, and we're all great sinners, next to a holy God, Jesus says, "the one who comes to Me I will certainly not cast out (John 6:37b). Won't you come to Jesus for forgiveness of your sin and thus, be adopted into God's family whereby you can call out to Him as your, "Abba. Father." Then you can begin to experience the truths of this book for yourself and teach them to your children for His glory.

Endnotes

Prologue

1. D. Martyn Lloyd-Jones, *Studies in the Sermon on the Mount*, vol. 2 (Grand Rapids, MI: Eerdmans Publishing Company, 1981), 202.
2. Dr. Allen Mawhinney, "Gospels Course Outline," (Reformed Theological Seminary, Oviedo, FL), 147.

Chapter 1

1. Robert A. Peterson, *Adopted by God* (Phillipsburg, NJ: P&R Publishing Company, 2001), 7.
2. Dr. Steven L. Childers, "Introduction to Evangelism-The Message of Evangelism," (Reformed Theological Seminary, Oviedo, FL), 38.
3. Peterson, *Adopted by God*, 27.
4. Ibid., 37-38.

Chapter 2

1. Mawhinney, "Gospels Course Outline," 140.
2. Ibid., 141.
3. Ibid.

Chapter 3

1. W. Clarkson, *The Pulpit Commentary*, vol. 10, "Isaiah," vol. II (Grand Rapids, MI: Eerdmans Publishing Company, 1981), 496.
2. Ibid.
3. Charles Spurgeon, *The Treasury of David*, vol. 3 (Grand Rapids, MI: Baker Book House, Reprinted 1984), 265-266.
4. Charles Stanford, "Central Truths," 1859, *The Treasury of David*, vol. 3, 282.

Chapter 4

1. Lloyd-Jones, *Studies in the Sermon on the Mount*, vol. 2, 195.
2. William Barclay, *The Gospel of Matthew*, vol. 1 (Philadelphia: The Westminster Press, 1975), 270.
3. William Hendriksen, *The Gospel of Matthew* (Grand Rapids, MI: Baker Book House, 1973), 361.
4. Ibid., 362.
5. Ibid.
6. Barclay, *The Gospel of Matthew*, 271.
7. Ibid.
8. Ibid.
9. Gardiner Spring, *The Mercy Seat* (Morgan, PA: Soli Deo Gloria Publications, Reprint of 1863 edition), 48.
10. Haddon W. Robinson, "Our Daily Bread," vol. 47, no. 2 (Grand Rapids, MI: Radio Bible Class Ministries Devotional), May 10, 2002.
11. Joanie Yoder, "Our Daily Bread," vol. 47, no. 1, April 2, 2002.
12. Ibid.
13. John R. Rice, editor, *The Sword Scrapbook* (Murfreesboro, TN: Sword of the Lord Publishers, 1969), 13.
14. Mike Singletary, "Men's Devotional Bible Calendar," (Grand Rapids, MI: Zondervan Publishing House, 1993), November 12.
15. Rice, *The Sword Scrapbook*, 13.
16. Singletary, "Men's Devotional Bible Calendar," December 17.

Chapter 5

1. Leon Morris, *The Expositor's Bible Commentary, Hebrews* (Grand Rapids, MI: Zondervan Publishing House, 1996), 136.
2. Simon J. Kistemaker, *New Testament Commentary, Hebrews* (Grand Rapids, MI: Baker Books, 1984), 372.
3. Ibid.
4. R. C. H. Lenski, *The Interpretation of the Epistle of Hebrews* (Augsburg, 1961), taken from Geoffrey B. Wilson, *Hebrews* (Edinburgh: The Banner of Truth Trust, 1979), 175.
5. Alistair Begg, *Made For His Pleasure* (Chicago: Moody Press, 1996), 119.
6. Geoffrey B. Wilson, *Hebrews* (Edinburgh: The Banner of Truth Trust, 1979), 175.
7. Thomas Lye, "Explanatory Notes and Quaint Sayings," *The Treasury of David*, vol. 4, 185.
8. Robert Traill, *The Works of Robert Traill*, vol. 2 (Edinburgh: The Banner of Truth Trust, Reprinted 1975), 284.
9. John Colquhoun, *Spiritual Comfort* (Morgan, PA: Soli Deo Gloria Publications, Reprint of 1814 edition), 219.
10. Philip Hughes, *Commentary on the Epistle to the Hebrews* (Grand Rapids, MI: Eerdmans Publishing Company, 1977), 528.
11. Begg, *Made For His Pleasure*, 119.
12. Ibid.
13. Lewis Bayly, *The Practice of Piety* (Morgan, PA: Soli Deo Gloria Publications, Reprint of 1842 edition), 273.
14. Charles Bridges, *Commentary on Proverbs*, taken from Wilson, *Hebrews*, 176.
15. Wilson, *Hebrews*, 177.
16. Ibid., 177-178.
17. Morris, *The Expositor's Bible Commentary*, 138.
18. Ibid.
19. Wilson, *Hebrews*, 176.
20. Don Kistler, "Sola Scriptura", The Theological Publication of Soli Deo Gloria Ministries, vol. 6, no. 4, Winter 1992, 4.

21. Spring, *The Mercy Seat*, 150.
22. Kistler, "Sola Scriptura", 4.
23. Rice, *The Sword Scrapbook*, 15,50.
24. Ibid., 31.
25. Kistler, "Sola Scriptura", 6.
26. Ibid., 5.
27. Ibid., 6.
28. Ibid., 8.
29. Ibid., 6.
30. Rice, *The Sword Scrapbook*, 113.
31. Kistler, "Sola Scriptura", 14.

Chapter 6

1. William Morris, Editor, *The American Heritage Dictionary of the English Language* (New York: American Heritage Publishing Co., Inc., 1970), 1320.
2. Ibid.
3. Ibid.
4. J. N. D. Kelley, *A Commentary on the Pastoral Epistles*, taken from Fritz Rienecker, *A Linguistic Key to the Greek New Testament* (Grand Rapids, MI: Zondervan Publishing House, 1976), 647.
5. J. Vernon McGee, *Thru The Bible Series, The Epistles, 1&2 Timothy, Titus, Philemon* (Nashville: Thomas Nelson Publishers, 1991), 122.
6. Morris, *The American Heritage Dictionary of the English Language*, 1320.
7. Rienecker, *A Linguistic Key to the Greek New Testament*, 647.
8. J. J. Van Oosterzee, *The Pastoral Epistles, The Second Epistle of Paul to Timothy*, taken from D. Edmond Hiebert, *Second Timothy* (Chicago: Moody Press, 1958), 102.
9. Jerome H. Smith, *The New Treasury of Scripture Knowledge* (Nashville: Thomas Nelson Publishers, 1992), 1435.
10. James Dobson, "Men's Devotional Bible Calendar", January 10.
11. Kistler, "Sola Scriptura", 14.
12. Rice, *The Sword Scrapbook*, 91.

13. Kistler, "Sola Scriptura", 14.
14. Ibid.
15. Rice, *The Sword Scrapbook*, 77.
16. Kistler, "Sola Scriptura", 14.
17. Ibid.
18. Rice, *The Sword Scrapbook*, 35.
19. Kistler, "Sola Scriptura", 10-11.
20. "Operation Timothy", Book Two (Christian Businessmen's Committee, Chattanooga, TN., 1980), 32.
21. Dr. Bruce Waltke, "Judges to Poets", Lecture 12 (Reformed Theological Seminary, Oviedo, FL, Spring 2002), 5.

Chapter 7

1. Leon Morris, *Tyndale New Testament Commentaries, The Gospel According to St. Luke* (Grand Rapids, MI: Eerdmans Publishing Company, 1982), 237.
2. G. Campbell Morgan, *The Gospel According to Luke* (Old Tappen, NJ: Fleming H. Revell Company, 1931), 181.
3. Morris, *Tyndale New Testament Commentaries, The Gospel According to St. Luke*, 240.
4. Ibid.
5. Kenneth E. Bailey, "The Pursuing Father", *Christianity Today*, October 26, 1998, 35.
6. Ibid.
7. Ibid.
8. Ibid., 35-36.
9. Frederic Louis Godet, *Commentary on Luke* (Grand Rapids, MI: Kregel Publications, 1981), 376.
10. Alfred Edersheim, *The Life and Times of Jesus the Messiah*, Part Two (Grand Rapids, MI: Eerdmans Publishing Company, 1971), 260.
11. Norval Geldenhuys, *The New International Commentary on the New Testament, The Gospel of Luke* (Grand Rapids, MI: Eerdmans Publishing Company, 1983), 407.

12. A. T. Robertson, *Word Pictures in the New Testament*, vol. II (Grand Rapids, MI: Baker Book House, 1930), 209.
13. Rienecker, *A Linguistic Key to the Greek New Testament*, 187.
14. Edersheim, *The Life and Times of Jesus the Messiah*, Part Two, 261.
15. William Barclay, *The Daily Study Bible Series, The Gospel of Luke* (Philadelphia: The Westminster Press, 1975), 205.
16. Godet, *Commentary on Luke*, 377.
17. Bailey, "The Pursuing Father", 38.
18. Ibid.
19. Tom Carter, *Spurgeon at His Best* (Grand Rapids, MI: Baker Book House, 1988), 286.
20. Joseph Alleine, *An Alarm to the Unconverted* (Carlisle, PA: The Banner of Truth Trust, Reprinted in 1959 from the first publication in 1671), 131.
21. Bailey, "The Pursuing Father", 38.
22. Ibid.
23. Barclay, *The Daily Study Bible Series, The Gospel of Luke*, 205.
24. Ibid.
25. Stephen Charnock, "Explanatory Notes and Quaint Sayings", *The Treasury of David*, vol. 4, 467.
26. Stephen Charnock, *The Existence and Attributes of God*, vol. 1 (Grand Rapids, MI: Baker Book House, 1979), 489.
27. Thomas Adams, "Explanatory Notes and Quaint Sayings", *The Treasury of David*, vol. 4, 468.
28. John MacArthur, Jr., *The MacArthur New Testament Commentary, Galatians* (Chicago: Moody Press, 1987), 178-179.
29. Christopher Love, *The Dejected Soul's Cure* (Morgan, PA: Soli Deo Gloria Publications, Reprinted in 2001, first published in 17th century), 103.

Chapter 8

1. Jeremiah Burroughs, *The Saint's Treasury* (Morgan, PA: Soli Deo Gloria Publications, reprinted 1991 from 1656 sermons), 136.
2. Ibid., 137.

3. Dave Branson, "Our Daily Bread", vol.47, no. 6, September 4, 2002.
4. Adams, "Explanatory Notes and Quaint Sayings", *The Treasury of David*, vol. 4, 468.
5. Rice, *The Sword Scrapbook*, 127.

Chapter 9

1. Spiro Zodhiates, *The Complete Word Study Dictionary, New Testament* (Chattanooga, TN: AMG Publishers, 1993), 64.
2. "The Dave Roever Story," cassette tape, Roever Evangelistic Association, PO Box 136130, Fort Worth, TX 76136.
3. G. Rawlinson, *The Pulpit Commentary*, vol. 10, "Isaiah," vol. II, 232.
4. La Leche League International, *The Womanly Art of Breastfeeding* (New York: Penguin Books, Fourth Edition, 1987), 71-72, 81-83.
5. Rice, *The Sword Scrapbook*, 140.
6. Ibid.
7. R. Tuck, *The Pulpit Commentary*, vol. 10, "Isaiah," vol. II, 246.
8. Ibid.
9. Spring, *The Mercy Seat*, 49.
10. Yoder, "Our Daily Bread," vol. 46, no. 12, March 6, 2002.
11. Thomas Watson, *The Lord's Prayer* (Carlisle, PA: The Banner of Truth Trust, Revised edition, 1965 from the 1890 edition), 13.
12. Rice, *The Sword Scrapbook*, 75.
13. Singletary, "Men's Devotional Bible Calendar," November 12.
14. David McCasland, "Our Daily Bread," vol. 47, no. 8, November 28, 2002.

Chapter 10

1. Ezekiel Hopkins, *The Works of Ezekiel Hopkins*, vol. 2 (Morgan, PA: Soli Deo Gloria Publications, Reprint of 1874 edition), 366.
2. Ibid., 368.
3. Wilson, *Hebrews*, 98.
4. Yoder, "Our Daily Bread", vol. 47, no. 2, May 24, 2002.

5. R. Kent Hughes, *Hebrews: An Anchor For the Soul*, vol. 1 (Wheaton, IL: Crossway Books), 208.
6. John MacArthur, Jr., *The MacArthur New Testament Commentary, Romans 1-8* (Chicago: Moody Press, 1991), 466.
7. A.T. Robertson, *Word Pictures in the New Testament*, vol. IV, 377.
8. James Montgomery Boice, *Romans, Volume 2, The Reign of Grace* (Grand Rapids, MI: Baker Book House, 1992), 890.
9. Ibid., 898.
10. Waltke, "Judges to Poets," Lecture 13, 9.
11. Boice, *Romans, Volume 2, The Reign of Grace*, 899.
12. Rice, *The Sword Scrapbook*, 146.
13. Ibid., 49.

Epilogue

1. David McCasland, "Our Daily Bread", vol. 47, no. 10, January 14, 2003.
2. Rice, *The Sword Scrapbook*, 110.
3. Kistler, "Sola Scriptura", 12.
4. Rice, *The Sword Scrapbook*, 46.
5. Singletary, "Men's Devotional Bible Calendar", March 28.
6. Steve Farrar, "Men's Devotional Bible Calendar", March 11.

www.ingramcontent.com/pod-product-compliance
Lightning Source LLC
Chambersburg PA
CBHW030319080526
44584CB00012B/633